The Forgotten Touch

The Forgotten Touch

More Stories of Healing

NIGEL W. D. MUMFORD

SEABURY BOOKS
An imprint of Church Publishing, Inc., New York

Published in the United States of America by Church Publishing, Inc.
No portion of this book may be reproduced, stored in or introduced
into a retrieval system, or transmitted, in any form or by any means,
including photocopying, without the prior written permission of
Church Publishing, except in the case of brief quotations embedded
in critical articles and reviews.

Library of Congress Cataloging-in-Publication Data
Mumford, Nigel.
    The forgotten touch : more stories of healing / Nigel W. D.
Mumford.
        p.   cm.
    ISBN-13: 978-1-59627-066-4 (pbk.)
    1. Mumford, Nigel. 2. Healers—England—Biography.
    3. Christian biography—England. 4. Spiritual healing.
    5. Healing—Religious aspects—Christianity. I. Title.
    BT732.56.M85A3 2007
    234'.131—dc22   2007023525

Scripture quotations are from the *New International Version* and the
New Revised Standard Version of the Bible.

Printed in the United States of America.

Church Publishing, Incorporated
445 Fifth Avenue
New York, New York 10016
www.churchpublishing.org

    5 4 3 2 1

To my dear wife
LYNN
who has encouraged and supported me in writing this book,
who has driven me home after so many healing services and
healing missions when there is nothing left in me to give,
and who has witnessed the joys of answered prayer
and the sorrows of the ultimate healing.

And to my oldest and dearest friend
WILLIAM QUAYLE
1954 – 2007
whom I knew since we were five months old. We had such fun
as kids and always picked up our friendship whenever we were
together over the past fifty-three years. Unfortunately William
smoked for thirty-eight years and at the end had to drink liquid
morphine even to eat. He would want to say, "Please don't smoke,"
and I would agree. We lost a true friend because of cigarettes.

Contents

Acknowledgments

I would like to thank Cynthia Shattuck for pulling this book together and Vicki Black for her amazing editing. The editing process can be so stressful but Vicki made it so easy—so much so that I want to write another book! Thank you, Vicki. What a joy it has been working with you both. Thank you.

Foreword

by the Rev. Dr. Russ Parker, MTh.
Director, Acorn Christian Healing Foundation

Someone once said that a testimony is worth a thousand sermons. Undoubtedly sermons can inspire and challenge, but testimonies tell us that God is on the loose and doing wonderful and stunning things among us today. They are powerful reminders that God wants to touch us, too; they are also disturbing challenges, because they invite us to come close to God so that he can come close to us.

So take a deep breath and get ready to be stimulated and surprised when you read this book. Nigel Mumford tells us his own story of how God stepped out of heaven and into his life and turned his world and his heart upside down. It is an honest story of an ordinary man—not a superstar whom God could not have failed to pick up and use so effectively. For me, this is its central attraction, because so many of us cancel ourselves out of being used by God precisely because we know that we are not extraordinary. What a waste of a life that is! Nigel's story echoes the words of another modern pioneer of Christian healing, John Wimber, the co-founder of the Vineyard churches, who said of the healing ministry: "Everybody gets to play!"

This book is full of healing stories that will open your mind towards God. There is also autobiography, as Nigel tells his own story of his journey to faith in Christ, and his call to pray with others for healing. He tells of God's generosity and grace in his life. In this book he expands more fully on his life story than he did in his first book, *Hand to Hand*. Along the way he admits his mistakes (so good to have this unashamedly shared in a book full of miracles!) and he is open about the fact that he doesn't have all the answers as to why some people are healed and others are not. He acknowledges those who have mentored and helped him to become the person of faith that he is.

A third and most valuable theme of the book is a practical guide to a host of healing needs and situations, both in congregations and other places of prayer, all of which offer clear teaching laced with good Brit humour and frankness.

I think Nigel's heart is to see people healed and to empower people to be a channel of healing for others. He is not seeking a following, but rather a way to help us follow the healing Jesus into an adventure of his choosing and empowering.

So I heartily commend Nigel's new book as a wonderful tribute to the faithfulness of the God he adores and a timely reminder of the power of God to heal through anyone who, like Nigel, says to God, "Here am I, Lord. Use me if you will." I find that if we pray that prayer, God usually does. So go on now and read this book, pray that prayer, and get ready for the healing adventure that is surely going to follow!

Prologue

"For I know the plans I have for you," declares the LORD, "plans to prosper you and not to harm you, plans to give you hope and a future. Then you will call upon me and come and pray to me, and I will listen to you. You will seek me and find me when you seek me with all your heart. I will be found by you," declares the LORD, "and will bring you back from captivity." (Jeremiah 29:11–14)

To encourage and guide others into prayer for healing is the very call upon my life. In the Bible we are told not to keep silent about the wondrous acts of our healing and forgiving God: "Brothers [and sisters], if you have a message of encouragement for the people, please speak" (Acts 13:15). That is what this book is all about: it is a message of encouragement for the people. It is a book to encourage others to pray and to have faith that when we seek the Lord with all our heart, we will indeed find the healing God who frees us from all that holds us captive. In so many places the Bible encourages us to share what the Lord is up to in our lives. The psalmist sang, "Give thanks to the LORD, call on his name; make known among the nations what he has done. Sing to him, sing praise to him; tell of all his wonderful acts" (Psalm 105:1–2). We need to *tell* people when we have experienced healing or witnessed the healing of others. People need to know that God heals today, that "Jesus Christ is the same yesterday and today and forever" (Hebrews 13:8).

My first book, *Hand to Hand: From Combat to Healing,* tells the story of my journey from my years as a drill instructor in the military to my call to be a minister of healing, as well as stories of God's healing grace. This book continues that story of God's marvelous power to heal today. As I have prayed with people over many years now, I have found that good mentors are essential in the process of growing into maturity in the healing ministry, a ministry that is often handed on through oral tradition. At every step of the way God has provided the mentors I have needed, just when I needed them. Their teachings, faith, and example permeate the pages of this book, and I thank God for them.

My first mentor was Avery Brooke, a wonderful and wise woman who for a number of years guided and pointed me in the right direction every six weeks or so. Francis and Judith MacNutt and Tommy Tyson were instrumental in molding me as I listened to their teaching. When it became obvious that I was being called to the healing ministry Francis would often question me, "Nigel, are you in this for the sprint or the long distance race?" He would also remind me to "Respond to the Spirit, not the need." Two valuable snippets of instruction I have relied on for many years. Other mentors come to mind: Russell Parker, a man of extraordinary gifts and insight who is clearly called to "preach the kingdom and heal the sick." Ellen Tillotson, David Maguire, Herbert Sanderson, Daniel Herzog, and David Bena have generously listened to me at great length and have renewed my faith and courage as I have prayed for so many people enduring untold suffering and pain.

Canon Jim Glennon of the Diocese of Sydney in Australia was my main mentor for sixteen years. During his visits to the United States we often just sat and talked—well, he talked and I listened! He passed on to me information that Agnes Sanford had taught him. Canon Jim encouraged and actually empowered me for this ministry. Just as the mantle of God's healing power was passed from Elijah to Elisha (2 Kings 2:15), so Canon Jim handed over to me the baton of a healing ministry to my generation. In a letter that I will always treasure he wrote, "It is distressingly true that people soon forget the insights of the healing ministry if they do not have constant input, and God raises up people in every generation to provide that input, such as you are now giving and Agnes Sanford gave in her own lifetime. Francis MacNutt and I and others of course have sought to do this as we are able. So remember that God has called you to catch a torch in your own generation, and I warmly congratulate you on what you have so far done. To God be the glory." Canon Jim wrote the foreword to my first book, and the "fiery chariot" came for him in Australia on the very day I was ordained a deacon, June 11, 2005. God bless you, Canon

Jim. May you rest in peace. I miss not being able to pick up the phone and dial Australia. Now I just pray.

People read books on healing for a variety of reasons. Perhaps you are just curious. Perhaps you have an interest in helping others, and sense that God is calling you to the healing ministry. Perhaps you have seen fruits of the gifts of healing in your life and are shaking in your boots, wondering, "What are you doing with me, God?" Perhaps you have a diagnosis and need to be healed, or you need a good dose of hope in what looks like a hopeless situation. For whatever reason you are reading this book, turn to God and *ask*. Sometimes that is all it takes. Give God a chance to answer. Hand it all over to him, stand back, and then see what happens. "Here, God. This is the situation. I need your help." I do believe that handing everything over to God in faith and love—the call to healing prayer, the diagnosis or problem, the medications, the choice of the right doctor or specialist—is the first step in this mystery of healing.

So, for whatever reasons you have picked up this book, keep reading. Soak up the hopeful message that Christ has for you. Go on, step out of the boat. His hand is reaching out to help you.

PART ONE

God's Healing Grace

Praise be to the God and Father of our Lord Jesus Christ, the Father of compassion and the God of all comfort, who comforts us in all our troubles, so that we can comfort those in any trouble with the comfort we ourselves have received from God. For just as the sufferings of Christ flow over in to our lives, so also through Christ our comfort overflows.

(2 Corinthians 1:3–5)

CHAPTER 1

Witness to the Resurrection
Embracing a Ministry of Healing

Jesus said to Martha, "I am the resurrection and the life. He who believes in me will live, even though he dies; and whoever lives and believes in me will never die. Do you believe this?" (John 11:25–26)

D o you believe this? I do. Like those first disciples, I have been a witness to the resurrection: the resurrection of the forgotten touch of the healer, Christ. I am a former Royal Marine Commando drill instructor. I am a man who has spent a full year in combat, has been shot at three times and blown up at bomb sites five times. I have drowned, suffered shell shock, and struggled mightily with my faith. But I am also a man who has been transformed and indeed resurrected from the pit of discouragement and depression. Resurrection comes in many forms: the resurrection of hope that God is truly listening, the resurrection of knowing that prayer is truly answered in the form of healing in all areas of our life. I am privileged to be a witness to this resurrection of the forgotten touch in my life and in the lives of others.

My call to the healing ministry came shortly after my sister, Julie Sheldon, formerly a dancer with the London Royal Ballet, was healed from a neurological disease called dystonia. Dystonia causes full body convulsions, and Julie was not expected to live long: the doctors feared she would break her own neck during a particularly severe attack. Her dancing career was destroyed by the disease, but after she was completely and miraculously healed of that devastating condition she encouraged many others by telling the story of her healing in her book *Dancer Off Her Feet*. In witnessing her healing by prayer, my life was changed. Totally changed. Absolutely transformed. Since that healing I have dedicated my life to the healing ministry.

There are so many facets of the human being that need to be healed. Physical, emotional, mental, spiritual, and even generational issues can be handed down through the family tree, both good and bad. I believe it is helpful in trying to understand who we are in looking at one's life story and then looking at God and combining the two. In this way we can all see the healing touch of Christ in our lives, and know that we are indeed witnesses to the resurrection.

To look back on my life and see the hand of God at work is truly amazing. Life has led me from being a drill instructor in Her Majesty's Royal Marine Commandos to becoming an ordained minister with a passion for the ministry of healing. The Roman Catholic priest Henri Nouwen wrote about the pastor as a "wounded healer," and surely I qualify for that position! As I look back on my life I see many dark nights of my soul, as well as the shining grace of Christ the healer. I thank God for his healing presence in my life.

At the age of seven Winston Churchill was told by his boarding school teacher, "You are useless and will amount to nothing." He was humiliated in front of his class. At the age of seven, at Plymouth College prep school, I had the same experience. I still remember it as if it just happened; I can feel the teacher's frustration coming at me in anger as he bellowed, "Mumford, you're useless, and you will amount to nothing." I felt that I had a tattoo on my arm that proclaimed: Dunce. A very deep wound pierced my heart right then. Children are so malleable and can be hurt so easily. The humiliation of that day has built up into layer upon layer of scar tissue in my life. Yet just as Churchill was released of that curse as he saved a nation at war, so I have been healed through the ministry of introducing people to the gospel of healing, one at a time. Much of the ministry I witness is in healing such wounds of the past in inner healing or the healing of memories. Christ heals even the scar tissue of life.

The scars of my experience of combat are both physical and emotional. I remember the gaping wound above my left eye that poured so much blood I could not see, the bucket of human excrement that was poured over my head, the three bullets that narrowly missed my head and groin. I can still hear the bombs that deafened me and in one case threw me violently backward into a door, where I crumpled to the ground, counting my fingers and checking for blood in my ears. My mind was tormented with shell shock after four of my recruits were killed in combat.

The wound of divorce is also part of my life story, when seventeen years of marriage ended rather abruptly and, from my perspective, out of the blue. Those who have gone through the pain of ripping one's heart apart know that divorce is a living hell for several months or indeed for some years. But even in the midst of such devastation God was gently and quietly present, as people who had been divorced came out of the woodwork and stood by me. They understood, and their prayers helped me through the very painful transition. For several years I was single. Judith MacNutt prayerfully told me, "Nigel, you are ready but the woman God has for you is not. Have patience and wait on the Lord; she will be revealed." Judith was right on the mark. I waited. The woman I was going to marry was not ready. She was going through a divorce herself!

In November 1996 the bishop of the Episcopal Diocese of Connecticut installed me as the director of the Oratory of the Little Way on a dark and stormy night when four hundred people came through the rain. As the head usher (who, I might add, did not want to be there) swished up and down the aisle seating people, she caught my eye. After a while (five months, as Lynn likes to remind me!), I got up the courage to ask her out for a cup of coffee. She said yes—and the rest is history. As we learned after the wedding, my mother, who did not come to the installation, picked out Lynn in the video and said to my father, "That's the girl for my son." God is so good. I even have two adult step-children, Matthew and Megan, who have taught me so much.

Four years after we were married, I took Lynn to the Plymouth area of Devon, England, where I was brought up. It was so healing to visit the places of my childhood—including my old boarding school, where I went at seven years old and was so badly bullied. The building was for sale and no one was there. We walked around and I reminisced. We visited a couple of places where I had been deeply hurt, and we prayed.

I have been listening and praying for people since 1990, but I still get blindsided at the depth of human cruelty. After the horrors of 9/11, I was thrown into the deep end as I tried to help the people who had suffered so much. Many people who came to me had been at the World Trade Center that day, while many others were therapists who came for prayer suffering from compassion fatigue. All were seeking healing in so many ways, with most suffering in some way from post-traumatic stress disorder. My mother wisely said, "Nigel, God has recycled you." As a veteran of combat I have witnessed our inhumanity and cruelty to others, and now I have the privilege of witnessing God's healing touch.

The millstone hung around my neck after 9/11 nearly succeeded in dragging me under. Now I can see that all those dark nights of the soul were for a reason—basic training for life, living, and healing. Basic training in listening to others who have suffered. I thank God daily for his love for us and his gift of healing. There is hope and love and the light in his healing grace, of this I have no doubt whatsoever. The power of the Holy Spirit falls like a waterfall to help and heal people in need. What a privilege it is to hear the history of a soul and then observe God lifting the pain. What a joy it is to actually *see* someone change. What a gift it is to watch the smile on someone's face who has known God's healing grace follow the floods of tears and anguish.

The writing and publication of my first book, *Hand to Hand: From Combat to Healing,* was an extraordinary experience. The book took three years to write on my one day off each week, with much help from a friend. We spent six months editing the manuscript and then sent it to four publishers in the United Kingdom and four publishers in the United States. All the publishers in the UK wrote back and said that the book should be published in the USA. All the publishers in the USA said the book should be published in the UK. I considered going to Greenland!

I do not "do" rejection well, and at one point in frustration I physically lifted the manuscript into the air and offered it to God. "God," I shouted, "this is your book. If you want it published, you do it." In desperate perseverance I gave up and just handed it over to God. When we remember to hand it *all* over to God, when we can come to a place of complete trust with God, that is when things happen and prayers are answered. That is the fulcrum point. I was deeply worried and stressed until that point when I raised up the manuscript and gave it over to God. Then I let it go. Several weeks later, when I was walking out of church after the service, a man at the end of the very pew I had been sitting in approached me. "Nigel, you know my name but you do not know what I do," Frank Hemlin said. "That's true," I replied. "What do you do?" He responded, "I am the publisher for Church Publishing. Would you write a book on healing for the church?"

Time stopped. My jaw dropped as I looked at Frank in utter astonishment. In a quiet voice I replied, "I already have written a book on healing." A couple of weeks after I sent the manuscript to Frank, I got a letter saying that Church Publishing would publish the book. I am still in awe as to how this all came about. We sent manuscripts all over the UK and USA, but the answer was sitting right next to me. It was a miracle.

The other miracle is that through the publishing of my first book I was able to forgive the teacher who had put me down so long ago. On my birthday my wife handed me a present: a copy of *Hand to Hand,* hot off the press. I wept. "Mumford, you will amount to nothing" rattled in my mind. But then I was able to hear myself say, "How wrong you were, Mr. Teacher. I am not a failure. I am deeply loved and redeemed by God." Thank you, Jesus, for healing me.

After serving eight years at the Oratory of the Little Way in Gaylordsville, Connecticut, as a full-time lay minister of healing, I knew it was time to move, time to grow. One Tuesday afternoon after a healing service I had four phone calls out of the blue with offers of positions at healing centers or congregations in Florida, New York, Pennsylvania, and Connecticut. I was thrown into a tailspin. How could four opportunities suddenly arrive in the same afternoon? What are you up to, God? My wife and I began praying for discernment. I distinctly remember one person who prayed over us at that time and spoke words that changed our lives, though he was not aware that we were praying for discernment. "Nigel," he prayed, "I see you as a pot-bound plant." He was right on target. The time at the Oratory had been a most blessed time, but one afternoon God clearly said it was time to be repotted.

Through much prayerful tension and after visiting a couple of possible ministries it became clear to us where God was leading. The process of discernment can be traumatic, and it was a huge relief when the decision was made. As we crossed the border from Connecticut to New York in our car full of belongings, following the moving van, I remembered the words of Julian of Norwich, "All shall be well, and all shall be well, and all manner of things shall be well." I also heard words that were firmly planted in my soul: "Try less and trust more." It seemed God was saying, "I am transplanting you from a small pot to a bigger pot, and you have to rely on me."

To try less and trust in God more is the only way one can go in the healing ministry. Perhaps I had to prove myself and be redeemed from the classroom at seven to become a drill instructor. Once again in the healing ministry God has redeemed me and put me on a new path. Perhaps I am a late bloomer, or perhaps his healing grace has been working in so many ways within my life without my even knowing it. The publicity this ministry has received had been quite amazing, but I find that now I don't need to prove anything. I only need to be an example of the love of Christ the healer.

We arrived at Christ the King Spiritual Life Center on July 5, 2004. At that point it was only a building site, but we held our healing services at the Convent of St. Mary's on site until the healing chapel was completed. Hundreds of people have helped me in this healing ministry as I try to understand what concerns are plaguing the individuals who come to us for prayer and healing. After about a month at Christ the King I sat at my desk in a fog, overwhelmed with prayer requests. I was not sure where my boundaries were; I did not know the end of the field. I called my bishop for help. The bishop responded, "Nigel, I trust you, I trust the Holy Spirit. Get on with it." A few life-changing words, spoken to empower. The fog cleared, and I could see the boundaries more clearly. It is amazing how a couple of words can change a life.

The culmination of a lot of mentoring in the healing ministry came for me on December 17, 2005, at my ordination to the priesthood in the Episcopal Church. The chapel was full and there was such an outpouring of love.

After the service Bishop Dan commented that this was the first charismatic ordination he had attended! My friend Russ Parker popped over for the day from England to preach. During the ordination service the ordinand lies on the floor prostrate while prayers asking for the presence of the Holy Spirit are sung. I had asked many clergy what spiritual revelation came upon them as they lay on the floor face down. One friend of mine commented that his revelation was: "I will never have another Sunday off for the rest of my life." Not what I had expected! I did think of his amusing comment as I was kneeling down, but as I lay on the floor I saw a slide show of my life. It was not like what I had seen in Malta while I was under the waves drowning; it was a different kind of near-death experience. It was the death of the old self and the birth of the new. My ordination was another moment of experiencing God's healing touch, just as through my ministry of praying with others for healing I have also been privileged to be a witness to this resurrection in the lives of many other people.

CHAPTER 2

The Forgotten Touch
Jesus' Healing Ministry

*Jesus went throughout Galilee, teaching in their syn-
agogues, preaching the good news of the kingdom,
and healing every disease and sickness among the
people. News about him spread all over Syria, and
people brought to him all who were ill with various
diseases, those suffering severe pain, the demon-pos-
sessed, the epileptics and the paralytics, and he
healed them. (Matthew 4:23–24)*

A story is told that Thomas Aquinas called upon Pope
Innocent II once when the latter was counting a large
sum of money. "You see, Thomas," said the pope, "the
church can no longer say 'Silver and gold have I none.'"

"True, holy father," said Thomas, "and neither can she now say, 'Arise and walk.'"

There seems to be some truth to Thomas's reply: historically Christ's ministry of healing has struggled, seeing periods of revival and then apparently dying out. But I believe that things are changing. In recent decades we have seen a gentle and sustained revival, both among individuals and from within the body of the church. This renewal of an often shunned way of helping people is blooming in upstate New York and within other communities in the United States, Great Britain, and Canada. In these places faith has been uplifted and people have returned to heartfelt prayers for healing.

My dear friend Dr. Francis MacNutt gives a wonderful history of the strange relationship between the church and individuals who are called to a ministry of healing in his book *The Healing Reawakening* (formerly titled *The Nearly Perfect Crime: How the Church Almost Killed the Ministry of Healing*). We all know the saying "Don't kill the messenger," though the messenger whom God sent to help us all was killed two thousand years ago. History has a propensity to repeat itself, and I have witnessed far too many people shun the message of hope. We are just as threatened by this ministry as were the people who encountered Jesus the healer two thousand years ago. Threatened by a loving ministry of hope and caring—and, I might add, the fruit of answered prayer.

During the past two thousand years God clearly has appointed people who are gifted and called with a passion to the ministry of healing. Some contemporary names come to mind: Agnes Sanford, Emily Gardiner Neal, Katherine Kuhlman, Francis and Judith MacNutt, Jim

Glennon, Russell Parker. These and many others have clearly had certain gifts given by God, gifts that are visible because of the fruitfulness of their ministry. "You did not choose me," Jesus told his disciples, "but I chose you to go and bear fruit—fruit that will last. Then the Father will give you whatever you ask in my name" (John 15:16). He also said we will know who his true disciples are by their fruit—"By their fruit you will recognize them" (Matthew 7:16)—the fruit being answered prayer, healing, restoration, reconciliation, revival, renewal, resurrection, and cure. The key to this gift of healing is that it is rooted firmly in the ground of seeking first the kingdom of God and proclaiming the love of Christ.

In reading the gospels it is very clear that Jesus healed throughout his ministry. Many healings are recorded as Jesus went about his daily life. He was a model for preaching the kingdom and healing the sick. Sometimes he healed the sick and then preached the kingdom! Jesus got the attention of people in his actions and they were privy to an insight of things seen and unseen. After the seed of healing is planted, the roots are formed under the soil, unseen. Then when the seed is ready, it pops into view. "All by itself the soil produces grain—first the stalk, then the head, then the full kernel in the head" (Mark 4:28). So it is in healing prayer. The seeds of hope and healing are planted and God germinates them.

Jesus sent out his disciples "to preach the kingdom of God and to heal the sick" (Luke 9:2). Most churches do indeed preach the kingdom, but fewer heal the sick. We have accepted the first part of the command; why have we generally not accepted the second? What is it about human nature that can be so guarded in rejecting hope?

Are we rejecting the Christ again? This is not a book on how to *preach the kingdom*—there are many books and courses and programs where one can learn to do just that. But what about part two of the command of Jesus, to *heal the sick*? How do we do this, Lord? Where is our faith?

After spending years totally focused on the gospels and especially the healing stories of Jesus, in recent months I have ventured out into the book of the Acts of the Apostles. Here we see the early church struggling with how to live out the gospel of healing entrusted to them after the death and resurrection of the Lord. Take the story of the crippled beggar, for example, in Acts 3. Peter and John, now flying solo, experience the power to heal as Peter says in confidence and all holy boldness, "Silver or gold I do not have, but what I have I give you. In the name of Jesus Christ of Nazareth, walk" (3:6). That kind of faith and blessed assurance is so rare today; I pray daily for that kind of devotion and conviction. I do wonder what Peter and John were thinking when this miracle happened. They knew the master had gone, yet somehow was still with them and able to heal through them. What had changed?

In the early church we can see the fruits of Jesus' healing ministry experienced through the gifts God gave to the apostles and other ministers of healing. In Paul's first letter to the church in Corinth he gives us a glimpse of what these gifts were, and how the church experienced and ordered them in their common life.

Now to each one the manifestation of the Spirit is given for the common good. To one there is given through the Spirit the message of wisdom, to another the message of knowledge by means of the same Spirit, to another faith by the same Spirit, to another gifts of healing by that one Spirit, to another miraculous powers, to another prophecy, to another the ability to distinguish between spirits, to another the ability to speak in different kinds of tongues, and to still another the interpretation of tongues. (1 Corinthians 12:7–10)

Paul's reminder that all of these gifts are from the same Spirit, "given for the common good" is something to keep an eye on—ego at the expense of the well-being of the community is not welcome here! The list of gifts is daunting: wisdom, knowledge, faith, gifts of healing, miraculous powers, prophecy, distinguishing between spirits, speaking in tongues, and finally the interpretation of tongues. Paul summarizes: "All these are the work of one and the same Spirit, and he gives them to each one, just as he determines" (12:11). So it is God who decides who gets what and when.

Paul then goes on to explain the relationship among these gifts by comparing them to the physical body, which is made up of many parts:

The body is a unit, though it is made up of many parts; and though all its parts are many, they form one body. So it is with Christ. For we were all baptized by one Spirit into one body—whether Jews or Greeks, slave or free—and we were all given the one Spirit to drink. (1 Corinthians 12:12–13)

The parts of the body need each other in order to be whole: in other words, one eye sitting on a plate would be a problem! "But in fact God has arranged the parts in the body, every one of them," Paul tells the Corinthians, "just as he wanted them to be. If they were all one part, where would the body be? As it is, there are many parts, but one body" (12:18–20).

Paul then lists the "parts" of the body of Christ: apostles, prophets, teachers, workers of miracles, "those having gifts of healing" (note it says *gifts* in the plural), helpers, administrators, and those who speak "in different kinds of tongues." He asks, "Are all apostles? Are all prophets? Are all teachers? Do all work miracles? Do all have gifts of healing? Do all speak in tongues? Do all interpret?" The questions are left unanswered, but we infer that the answer is no. Now comes the crunch: "But eagerly desire the greater gifts" (12:28–31).

Do we desire to receive the "greater gifts"? Are we bold enough to ask for them? Do we have the faith to seek them with all our heart? There is a wonderful story of a man who dies and goes to heaven. St. Paul checks his intake form and then says, "I have ten minutes before the next person comes in. Come with me." The two walk the streets of heaven until they come to a huge warehouse. Paul leads the way, then stops in front of a shelf filled with wrapped parcels. The chap asks Paul, "What are these?" Paul replies, "These are the gifts God wanted to give you, but you never asked."

Throughout its history the church has recognized the fruits of the healing ministry as it appeared in certain people, who clearly have the gifts of healing mentioned in 1 Corinthians 12. But in another letter from the early church, the letter of James, we also see a wider approach to the ministry of healing.

> Is any one of you in trouble? He should pray. Is anyone happy? Let him sings songs of praise. Is any one of you sick? He should call the elders of the church to pray over him and anoint him with oil in the name of the Lord. And the prayer offered in faith will make the sick person well; the Lord will raise him up. If he has sinned, he will be forgiven. (James 5:13–15)

What do we do if we are in trouble? Pray. What do we do if we are happy? Sing praises. What do we do if we are sick? Call the leaders of the church and ask them to pray and anoint us with oil. Now here is the fruit: "Confess your sins to each other and pray for each other so that you may be healed" (5:16). This is perhaps a promise that some do not dare to believe. Confession plays a huge role here; healing is about letting go, totally handing it all over to God as we are forgiven.

Indeed certain people have specific gifts of healing, but here in James we see that we in the church are called to pray for the sick as a matter of course. Apparently we can *all* pray for each other, and as we pray for each other, the power of God will be present that we may be healed. As we confess our sins, as we let go of what controls us, as we come to realize that truly God heals today because Christ is the same yesterday, today, and forever, we experience how gentle, tender, straightforward, and kind this ministry of Christ is. We realize that healing is available for everyone, even—or especially—those who feel that they are not worthy.

This teaching in James finishes with a positive affirmation, one that we should all strive to live for: "The prayer of a righteous person is powerful and effective" (5:16). The prayers of a good, virtuous, just, blameless, upright, honorable, and honest person are influential, commanding, and effectual.

I am convinced we are seeing a resurrection of the forgotten touch in our generation. The resurrected hand that bears the scar of the nail is stretched forth to help and heal us in our time of need. This hand is offered in love and compassion; this hand conveys the authority and power to change lives, one by one. Do we have the courage to obey the Lord in preaching the kingdom and healing the sick? Are we bold enough to preach the message of the resurrection of the forgotten touch?

What is stopping you from praying for healing, either for yourself or for someone who needs God's healing touch? Embarrassment? Fear that your prayer will not work? Trepidation that your prayer *will* work? Rejection? Ponder that question as you read the stories of healing in this book. What is blocking you from stretching forth your hand?

CHAPTER 3

Out on a Limb

Moving Out of Our Comfort Zone

If anyone is in Christ, he is a new creation; the old has gone, the new has come! All this is from God, who reconciled us to himself through Christ and gave us the ministry of reconciliation. . . . We are therefore Christ's ambassadors, as though God were making his appeal through us. . . . As God's fellow workers we urge you not to receive God's grace in vain. For he says, "In the time of my favor I heard you, and in the day of salvation I helped you." I tell you, now is the time of God's favor, now is the day of salvation. (2 Corinthians 5:17–20, 6:1–2)

I became aware a few years ago that in order to pray for healing, either for yourself or for others, you have to go out on a limb—because that is where the fruit is! You have to leave your comfortable spot on the ground, hugging the safety of the solid tree, and crawl out on the branches. There are many times during a typical day I feel that I am totally out of my depth. Over and over I have to remind myself that I am not doing any of this alone. It is a divine partnership in which I am an ambassador of Christ and a witness to his resurrection life.

My wife and I went to a great gathering of the clans recently at the Scottish games in Altermont, New York. There was an *ad hoc* military unit and they had the FN 7.62 rifle on display. I had not touched one since 1978, and I very hesitantly picked up the weapon. The men in the unit had been trying to learn from a manual, so I did the "drill instructor thing" and showed the lads the drill. Afterward they all gathered around me and surprised me with a huge round of applause. It was strange to hold that rifle again; I realized it had been a "comfort" to carry "that thing" in combat, as it represented safety, life, and defense. Now I find that same comfort in carrying the Bible— safety, life, and love are so much more a part of me today. Interesting how God works!

The more experience I have with the healing ministry the more I see it as a call to get out of our comfort zone. Asking us to believe that healing is abundantly available today is like the Lord calling us daily to get out of the boat and by faith to walk on the water: "'Lord, if it's you,' Peter replied, 'tell me to come to you on the water.' 'Come,' he said" (Matthew 14:28–29). Often in our prayers we are guilty of limiting God, who can and *will* do "immeasurably more than all we ask or imagine" (Ephesians 3:20). God's work of healing is beyond our imagination; we have to think in a different way. We have to put on the "mind of Christ" (1 Corinthians 2:16) and think outside the box of our limitations. We are called to pray beyond our imagination, to dare to believe what we cannot understand, with an absolute trust in God. "I do believe; help me overcome my unbelief!" (Mark 9:24). Help us, Lord, to think and pray outside our comfort zone, outside the physical constraints of human life to which we have grown so accustomed. Help us to have the courage to step out onto the sea of faith, keeping our eyes on the Lord.

The Bible tells us that we need to "be prepared in season and out of season" (2 Timothy 4:2). We have to be ready to preach God's word of grace wherever we are in the midst of our everyday lives—even, as I discovered recently, when traveling or standing in line at the post office. The way the Lord surprises us with his healing touch is so wonderful. In eagerly desiring the greater gifts he is showing us a far more excellent way, the way of love and compassion that he had for fellow suffering human beings. If we actively seek the Lord and ask for his greater gifts of wisdom, knowledge, faith, and gifts of healing, lives can be renewed, restored, and healed, as the following stories powerfully show.

Since the healing ministry requires me to travel a lot, I sit next to many people on airplanes and pray that the Lord has put us together for a reason. Often the conversations are quite interesting. One day I was sitting next to a Roman Catholic nun who was on her way to Kyoto, Japan, to photograph the town for a Catholic magazine. We chatted for the entire length of the flight, she talking about her book and I talking about mine. When we started the descent to land she said, "Nigel, you have not asked me what is wrong with me." I shared that I do not normally ask people that question; they mostly tell me what they need prayer for. She then told me about the open wound on the heel of her foot that for months "would just not heal." She was concerned about doing a lot of walking in Kyoto on her painful foot, and asked if I would pray for her.

I said yes, and then had the shock of my life. Here we were, sitting packed together in an airplane, when suddenly this nun grabbed her foot and lifted her heel level with my chest (she must have been double-jointed!), right in front of my face, which was now inches from the weeping wound. It was not a pretty sight! The passengers on my left turned their heads in astonishment in our direction, their mouths falling open as they wondered what was going on across the aisle. I collected my thoughts, and with a foot in my face began to pray earnestly with faith for the healing of this nun's wound. It was a quick but powerful prayer!

We exchanged business cards (yes, the nun had a business card), and we each went our own way after collecting our luggage. Two weeks later I got an email from Kyoto that said, "Thank you, God, my heel was healed! I have been walking around Kyoto with a perfect ankle and no wound at all. Thank you, God." It was very much worth the embarrassment of a nun's foot in my face. God has a wonderful sense of humor.

Shortly after that flight I was waiting in a long line at the local post office. I was at the end of the line and knew that since people were sending Christmas packages it would take at least half an hour or more. I stood and prayed. The postmistress was having problems with a hand-held device that was not working properly. I watched her struggle with the electronic tool as it seemed to get worse and worse, slower and slower. Everyone was watching her as she got more embarrassed and frustrated with the device until it died. She spoke to it, she tapped it, she banged it, she hit it. Nothing. She was now frantic. Then she looked up and caught my eye. "Nigel!" she exclaimed in a very loud voice. "Come over here and fix this, will you?" She knew that I prayed for people and had seen hundreds of letters coming to us from all over the world. She was probably half-joking when she invited me to pray over an inanimate object, but I had nothing to lose so I stepped forward. I put my hand on the minicomputer and said a quiet prayer. Now I was the one who was a little embarrassed. But the postmistress picked up the machine, pushed the button to turn it on, and, well—guess what! The machine worked perfectly.

Everyone was relieved. The postmistress was so grateful. I paused, wondering if I was to go next in line after rendering such service! No such thing. I slowly walked back, not to where I left my place in the line, as

25

others now had joined it, but to the very end! I was even further back than when I came in. No one said a word. I was very surprised that the computer was working, but I was also a little surprised that no one said thank you or perhaps even noticed what had just happened. Justification came the next time I entered the post office, though. I was alone and the postmistress told me, with her hand on mine, that the machine had been playing up for some days just when she did not need it to act up, and that after the prayer it was fine and it was still working perfectly—and she then processed my mail with the thing. She was beaming from ear to ear and was so happy. She said, "Thank you," and I reminded her to thank God. God indeed works in strange and mysterious ways.

On a recent trip to England my brother Alec, my wife Lynn, and I had just finished strolling around the cathedral at Chichester in Sussex. I always feel that I have received a gift after making a pilgrimage to such a holy place, and we gave thanks as we left the grounds. We went and had a coffee and a pasty—my favorite! (The Cornish pasty, or oggy as we affectionately called it, was invented by the wives of Cornish tin miners. They are a full meal of meat and potato encased in pastry. Delicious!) We then went window shopping among the many small shops that make up that fortified Roman town.

My brother suddenly said with total conviction, "Let's go into this shop!" It was a woman's clothing shop; a trendy, music-blasting boutique. He thought that I should buy Lynn an "English present." Lynn and I were startled, but we went in and Lynn started looking around. She found a very fashionable, Twiggy-type, Carnaby Street pink hat. My brother told me it was "ten quid," so he and I went up to the two women at the checkout desk while Lynn kept shopping.

As we approached the desk, to embarrass me in true brotherly love, Alec announced to the woman that I was buying the pink hat for myself. I stopped dead in my tracks and gave him the look that only siblings can. One of the women said, "Oh, are you an actor?" We both laughed, and I said, "No, no, not really. Well, maybe a little. Standing in the pulpit does require some stage work!"

"What do you really do?" one asked. I told them I was studying to be a priest. That stopped them. "Oh, right. No, I mean, what do you *really* do?" she asked, thinking I was kidding. "Well, actually, I pray for sick people," I replied.

"Oh!" exclaimed the woman on my right. "I am very poorly." Much to our surprise, she then pulled up her T-shirt and pulled down the belt of her jeans to expose a wickedly pink operation scar that reached the full length of her belly. At this point my brother Alec literally squeaked and ran out of the building, completely embarrassed. The sales clerk told me she had been suffering with Crohn's disease, and that even after her recent surgery she still felt pain and discomfort due to scar tissue. I took out my Palm Pilot and asked for her name. "Sarah," she told me. I wrote it down and told her that I would be asking a lot of Americans to pray for her on the internet. She was deeply moved and very grateful. "You would really bother to do that?" she asked.

There was a pause, a holy pause, as if everything went quiet. Even the pop music seemed to fade out. I then knew that the Lord wanted me to lay hands on her. I asked her if she would like the laying on of hands. She said, "Do you think that God wants me to be well?" The other clerk and I assured her that it is indeed God's will that we be well. There was another holy pause and she looked at me intently as if to question me, and then very simply leaned forward from the hips over the counter, her body saying yes, please pray for me. I laid my hands on her head for quite a while and prayed. It was as if we were in a cocoon of healing grace, in the midst of all the other women shopping and bopping to the music. What a holy moment it was, a moment that came totally by surprise. We had brought the cathedral to her, as we were praying in the marketplace.

After I finished paying for the "trendy hat," I gave her my business card and told her that we would continue to pray for her. Just before Christmas I got a card from Sarah, thanking God for her healing. She had been back to her doctor and he had told her that she was healed and did not need to see him for a year. (She had been seeing the specialist on a weekly basis up to that point.) Sarah told me that when we prayed in the trendy boutique the pain had immediately stopped.

I confess that when I got that card from Sarah, tears freely fell down my cheek, I was so deeply moved. Lord, you never cease to amaze me; your plan is so wonderful. Help us to keep tuned into you, that we may be your ambassadors here on earth as you commanded us to preach the kingdom and heal the sick, and as we seek your greater gifts.

CHAPTER 4

Something *Always* Happens When We Pray

Stories of Healing

Jesus went down with them and stood on a level place. A large crowd of his disciples was there and a great number of people from all over Judea, from Jerusalem, and from the seacoast of Tyre and Sidon, who had come to hear him and to be healed of their diseases. Those troubled by evil spirits were cured, and the people all tried to touch him, because power was coming from him and healing them all. (Luke 6:17–19)

The question I am asked more than any other is, "Why are some people healed and others are not?" This is a very legitimate question, and a deep mystery of the healing ministry. I often respond by reframing that question as: "Why are some people healed and others are cured?" The dictionary defines "cure" as a recovery from disease or a remedy, while "heal" is defined as to make or become sound or whole. To be cured is to have a physical recovery from a disease; it is the remedy that restores someone to full health. To be healed, on the other hand, is to receive whatever is needed in order to become sound or whole; it is the emotional and spiritual release of disease. Both are the rectifying of an unhealthy or undesirable condition. I strongly believe that *everyone* receives a healing of some sort when we pray. Something *always* happens when we pray. God answers prayer in so many ways; the problem is that we often miss it! Perhaps after prayer there is less pain or less medication is needed; perhaps there is a closing of the gap between two people in a relationship. Perhaps the healing is so subtle that we miss the answer completely.

I do not know why everyone is not cured. I will not know that until I am at those pearly gates and can ask all my questions. Miracles happen in so many ways, from the amazing and mysterious to the subtle and quietly life-changing, from the spontaneous and immediate to the intentional and gradual. We do our part: we show up and do our best, and God does the rest. That is faith. We pray and pray and leave the outcome to God, trusting in the power and wisdom of our loving Lord to answer our prayers as may be best for us.

Recently at a large Fishnet Conference in Rutland, Vermont, I was about to introduce the speaker and "just had a feeling." I prayed, "Is this from you, God?" Then I heard myself say, in front of five hundred people, "God wants to heal right hips and hearing this week, apart from many other things." I have learned just to let it go and trust God when I receive these holy nudgings, though I could also rationalize that clearly from a percentage point of view, out of five hundred people several could have right hip problems and many might have hearing problems. Four days later I was asked to lead the testimony time at the end of the conference. I specifically asked about the word of knowledge that I had received at the beginning of conference. Five people had hips that had been healed, three people had hearing that had been healed, and one person had both a hip and hearing that had been healed. One person later wrote to the MacNutts a testimony, via Anne Early:

> While at the Fishnet Conference in Vermont this year, Nigel had a word of knowledge about someone's right hip being healed. Up until that night I suffered with pain in my right hip, especially while walking or any physical activity. I claimed my healing and I noticed that evening that the pain was gone. The following morning, same thing; later that night, no pain. Back home and on vacation still no pain, and as I type this out to you, yes, you're right, NO PAIN! Praise the Lord.

When my parents were in their early thirties, my father, David Mumford, slipped a disc in his back while reversing a tractor down a ramp from a big truck. After that he had much pain and discomfort. He consulted several doctors and osteopaths, was on bedrest, endured manipulation under anesthetic, and was put in a plaster jacket for three months—all to no avail. A spinal operation was agreed upon as a last resort.

One night, after my parents had retired for the night, my mother picked up Christopher Woodard's book *A Doctor Heals by Faith,* and was riveted. It was her first introduction to the Christian healing ministry and she read on into the night. Suddenly David woke up from his mattress bed on the floor and shouted, "There's a hand on my back!" My mother thought he was dreaming—he was on strong sedatives by then—but she jumped out of bed, knelt beside him, and took his hand to calm him. As soon as their hands touched they trembled, and then began to shake. She asked him why he was shaking—was he cold? He replied that he wasn't shaking, it must be her!

When they let go the shaking stopped, but when they joined their hands a second time it began again. Then they decided simply to be quiet and go along with it. Soon my parents were aware of a great peace between them and throughout the room. My mother remembers glancing over her left shoulder, thinking there was somebody there. Something was happening but it was beyond their understanding. Finally the shaking stopped and my father suddenly went into a deep sleep. My mother felt a bit forsaken and went back to bed, still trembling for some time. She picked up the book and continued reading until she fell asleep.

In the morning, David said he felt he could get up and stand without help—which he did without pain or even discomfort. They were astounded. He then proceeded to walk along the landing and back, saying, "It's better—it's gone," as my mother stood by in complete amazement. He washed and dressed himself totally unaided for the first time in many weeks. Up to this point my parents had known nothing of healing except through the medical profession. This healing was extraordinary—innocent, in the middle of the night, and almost instantaneous. The operation was cancelled. Now, forty years later, David has had no further trouble with his back.

My parents were left with the conviction that this healing was of God through his son Jesus Christ and in the power of the Holy Spirit. From that moment on, David has been drawn actively into the helping ministry of the Christian church. He has been an Anglican priest for twenty-seven years now, but this experience of Christ's healing was the beginning of it all.

In the following story of healing we see the same kind of faith the centurion had, who asked Jesus to heal his servant, who was paralyzed and in terrible suffering, simply by saying the word, without even praying or laying on hands. Jesus was amazed by the humility and faith of the centurion, and told the crowd, "I tell you the truth, I have not found anyone in Israel with such great faith" (Matthew 8:10). I heard this story told by one of the employees of Christian Healing Ministries (CHM) during the annual international board meeting in Jacksonville, Florida. I was seated at a formal dinner with Francis and Judith MacNutt, and when we heard the employee's story I sat there with my jaw open and tears running down my face. God does move in the most wonderful and mysterious ways.

The CHM team had been in Scotland to lead a healing mission for four hundred Presbyterian ministers. A woman had come all the way from London to give the testimony of healing about her son, a testimony of abundant faith. Some months before, this mother told the crowd, she had walked into a Christian bookstore in London and with her hands on her hips asked in a very loud voice, "Does anyone know anything about healing?"

Well, my father, the Rev. David Mumford, happened to be in the shop and went right up to the woman and told her that he certainly *did* know about the healing grace and love of the Lord. He asked her what needed healing in her life. She told my father that her son at seven had become bedridden; he was now twenty-one. He had been lying down for fourteen years with a debilitating sickness. "Nothing helped him," she loudly declared. My father stayed with her for some time, prayed, and then suggested several books that were on the shelf right in front of them: *Healing* by Francis MacNutt; *Dancer Off Her Feet, One Step at a Time,* and *The Blessing of Tears,* all by Julie Sheldon (his daughter and my sister!); and finally my first book, *Hand to Hand: From Combat to Healing.* She promptly brought all the books, and after another prayer said goodbye to my father.

She went home and read them all. She declared to the four hundred Scottish pastors that she read *Hand to Hand* last and then took the information at the back as a "recipe" for how to pray for her son—a word that made me smile. This woman of faith then prepared to "cook": she got an internet intercessor prayer group together to pray online. She gathered people to pray together every night for a week. She fasted, she asked people to pray. She was proactive and, not unlike the centurion, had faith beyond measure. Then when she felt all the "ingredients" were in the bowl, she asked her son if her prayer team could come and lay hands on him in his bedroom. They did. He got up. He was cured! Now that is what I call faith in God's healing presence. Pray for the gift of faith shown by the centurion and by this mother from London.

※

In his letter to the church in Ephesus, St. Paul encourages us to "think big" and to give all the glory to God, "who is able to do immeasurably more than all we ask or imagine, according to his power that is at work within us" (Ephesians 3:20-21). What is this "power"? The power of love, the power of faith, the power of trust. It is God's power and God's glory. The healing power of God can flow through us, yet far too often we are guilty of limiting that power. God can do "immeasurably more" than we can ask or even imagine. That tells me we need to pray more, with more faith and with more conviction, and to pray "bigger prayers" with our whole body, mind, and soul.

Over the course of two weeks some time ago, I learned an important lesson from God about healing prayer. I was leading our Tuesday weekly healing service and during the testimony time a man asked for prayer for his arthritic knees. I remember it well, as his knees were huge and very swollen. I laid my hands on his knees and the whole prayer team surrounded him during the service. I prayed a fervent prayer with everything I had. As I was praying with my eyes open (so I could see what God was up to!), I noticed the man starting to move his right shoulder. I asked, "What are you doing?" He replied, "My frozen shoulder has been healed." God was showing us that the ministry of healing prayer is much bigger than we know. Here we were praying a passionate and enthusiastic prayer for one thing, and a totally different thing happened. Another healing took place, thanks be to God. This is new, I thought; this is different.

The following week, at the next healing service, as if to make God's point very clear, another man sat in exactly the same pew as the man whose shoulder was healed. Just as happened the week before, this man too put up his hand during the testimonies and said that he wanted prayer for his "arthritic knees." His knees were swollen and pressing against his trouser legs. We all laid hands on this man and prayed a fervent, targeted, and passionate prayer that God would heal his arthritic knees. We finished our prayer and after a while he loudly proclaimed that the prayer had not been effective in the least. "Nothing happened," he shouted. "Nothing." Silence fell over the church. He was looking at me intently. What is going on here, God? I decided to assign a few members of the prayer team to keep praying for the man so that we could get on with the service. After the service he sarcastically commented again in the narthex on his way out, "Nothing happened." Over to you, God.

The next week the same man sat in the same pew. At the prayers before the service I was warned by the healing team that "he" was present. What is going on here, God? The service started, I smiled at the man, but no response. It was time for the testimonies. The man struggled to stand up. "Nigel," he said in a loud and dramatic voice, "You prayed for my arthritic knees last week." He paused for effect. "And nothing happened." Now there was an even longer pause. HELP, I prayed. I felt suspended in time, as if all my faith was being put to the test. What do I do now, God? The pause continued. We locked eyes and just looked at each other. It felt a bit like a shoot-out at the OK Corral. Who was going to draw first?

The man was having a bit of fun with me. A smile flickered on his face—I so wished the people in the congregation could see it! Finally he broke the silence in a much kinder voice. "Nigel, you prayed last week for my arthritic knees and nothing happened to them, but I need to tell you what did happen." Oh, thank you, God. "Nigel, I was healed of emphysema. I have been a smoker for years and I had emphysema for the past two years. I have been so sick, but I am totally healed. Thank you." The church erupted in joyous Amens and Hallelujahs. I stood there thanking God, now at last with a smile on my face. I had been taught a huge lesson in public: Nigel, don't limit God! Think bigger, pray bigger, pray with everything God has given you pray—and leave the answer to God.

❀

Perseverance is a word many do not want to hear in the process of healing, but sometimes it is exactly what is required. "You need to persevere so that when you have done the will of God, you will receive what he has promised," the letter to the Hebrews tells us (10:36). "Continue in prayer and watch in the same with thanksgiving," my mentor Canon Jim Glennon would repeat at almost every conversation we had. "Ask and it will be given to you; seek and you will find; knock and the door will be opened to you" (Matthew 7:7). How important it is to keep knocking on the door. Sometimes we have to be the squeaky wheel—squeak and you will receive the oil!

Carol taught me a lot about perseverance. She and her husband had been trying to conceive a child for several years since they got married. Carol came on most Wednesdays to the Oratory to receive prayers for conception and a healthy child. She took the train from New York, and someone had to pick her up. She kept coming, we kept praying, she and her husband kept trying. Nothing. Since she was not comfortable with the prayer team praying for her, it always had to be me, and I have to confess that I was becoming worn down and a little exasperated by the persistence and perseverance of this woman. Her situation threw me. God, why is Carol not conceiving? Is it the lack of my faith? She certainly had an abundance of it! She knew what she wanted—a healthy baby—and nothing was going to stop her.

One day I went to my spiritual director and unloaded. "I am at the end of my rope with this case," I blurted. My spiritual director laughed. Not the response I expected. "I am not sure that you understand the tension of this particular case." She laughed even more. "Are you really listening to me?" Now I was getting upset. "Nigel, calm down," she said. "I need to remind you of the Bible story of the persistent widow and the unjust judge. You are acting like the unjust judge. Where is your faith?" Ouch. This is why we all need to have accountability in our lives.

After the session with my spiritual director I felt humbled and redirected, and I confess somewhat embarrassed. I had totally missed what was going on. I called Carol and asked her to come to the Oratory the next Wednesday. She did, and I confessed my stress over her situation and asked Carol to forgive me. She did so with a wonderful smile. I suggested we pray some more.

Nine months later she gave birth to a very healthy boy. She called again eighteen months later and asked for more prayer, as they would like to have another child and were again having problems conceiving. This time I was ready and knew what to do! More faith, Mumford! The faith of the people who are praying is so important in the mysterious process of healing. Thank you, Carol, for that lesson in faith and for your forgiveness. We thank God for Carol's two healthy children.

It takes courage and fortitude to persevere in faith and to believe in the face of aridity and disappointment. "Now faith is being sure of what we hope for and certain of what we do not see" (Hebrews 11:1). Some time ago I had a phone call from a medical doctor and his wife who had been trying to conceive for eleven years and had had several miscarriages. We chatted and I suggested that they come to see us at the healing center. I remember the prayer session vividly. We entered the chapel and talked about the history of the situation. Then I felt the Lord nudge: it is time to pray. I had the couple lie face down on the floor, side by side but in a "V" so that I could kneel between them. I laid my hands on their lower backs and prayed and prayed for new life. I prayed that the womb would be ready and would carry to full-term, and that the fruit of the womb would be a very healthy child. I was very specific.

Someone once said, "You have to be careful what you pray for." Very shortly after their visit I had an excited phone call from the doctor's wife. "I'm pregnant," she announced. Hearing about an answer to prayer is so exciting, I still get a euphoric feeling of utter awe, joy, and love. Thank you, God. She then told me that there were three growing embryos in her womb. After eleven years of disappointments and perseverance in the face of loss, God answered the prayers of this couple in great abundance.

Kelly, Paige, and Lee were born the day before my birthday. I learned of their birth by a fax that came through with three sets of very small footprints. I stood at that machine and wept tears of joy. I smile every time I think of these three beautiful girls and their faithful and persevering parents.

Were the healings described in these stories the work of God? The power of suggestion? Mind over matter? Call it what you will, the bottom line is people experience healing when they choose to believe and to open themselves to receive God's power and grace. The healing may not be instantaneous and it may take time; the answer could be yes, no, or later; but I am convinced, *absolutely* convinced, after many years of convincing from God, that something *always* happens when we pray. The words Jesus said to his disciples apply to us as well: "Again, I tell you that if two of you on earth agree about anything you ask for, it will be done for you by my Father in heaven. For where two or three come together in my name, there am I with them" (Matthew 18:19–20). We can depend on it.

CHAPTER 5

The Great Physician
Healing Through Medicine

*My child, when you are ill, do not delay, but pray to
the Lord, and he will heal you. Give up your faults
and direct your hands rightly, and cleanse your heart
from all sin. Offer a sweet-smelling sacrifice, and a
memorial portion of choice flour, and pour oil on
your offering, as much as you can afford. Then give
the physician his place, for the Lord created him; do
not let him leave you, for you need him. There may
come a time when recovery lies in the hands of physicians, for they too pray to the Lord that he grant
them success in diagnosis and in healing, for the sake
of preserving life. (Sirach 38:9–14)*

Far too often we have seen Christian healing and the healing provided by the medical community as separate and distinct. In recent decades, though, we increasingly hear people affirm that healing is "both/and": it is found in both the medical community and the church, it involves both the individual with faith and the medical personnel who see their expert care as part of the resurrection of the forgotten touch. As someone once said, "Prayer and Prozac!" Dr. Lisa Thorn once commented to me, "In this world of MRIs, CT scans, blood work, and so on, it is so easy to forget the power of touch. I am reminded of this in reading your work and it helps when I am examining patients. The more experienced (read: older) I get in doing what I do, the more crucial I find intuition and palpation (the technical term for touch!) in diagnosing." It is very important that the Christian healing ministry is offered in conjunction with the medical profession. We never suggest that anyone cease taking their medication or go contrary to the advice of their physician. When prayer and medicine go hand in hand, the combined protocol can be very powerful. When we find a Christian doctor and a Christian prayer team working together, we see miracles happen.

One analogy I have found useful in describing the healing ministry is a set of railroad tracks: one rail is the finest medical expertise and treatment available to us; the other rail is the spiritual and faith dimension; and the third rail is the power of the Holy Spirit to bring about healing. If we take any one of the rails away, the train will not run. We need all three, as the following stories clearly show.

At school I was very shy. If the teacher asked me a question I would freeze, even if I knew the answer. I hated standing up and reading in front of the class. I went to a boy's boarding school from the age of seven to eleven; at eleven there were girls in my class, which was even more embarrassing! Most people have an inherent fear of public speaking. I can tell you that I did...off the charts.

So when I was asked to speak at Johns Hopkins Hospital, the largest hospital in the world, at a conference for four hundred physicians and hospital chaplains on complementary medicine, needless to say I was a bit nervous. I sat in the large hall filled with people, trying to breathe. I heard the master of ceremonies introduce me but my mind was fixed on the stairs to the podium. There were a lot of steps; what if I tripped and fell? After the introduction I walked slowly and trembling toward the stand. I looked down to check my footing. "Oh, God, why have you asked me to do this? HELP!" Then I glanced at my name tag, which read: "Nigel Mumford, Faculty, Johns Hopkins Hospital." I started to laugh. One minute I am shouting at recruits on the parade ground and then somehow I am on the faculty of Johns Hopkins? How can people say there is no God? By the time I reached the podium I was calm. I opened my mouth and the Lord's words came out. Thanks be to God.

I was given half an hour to talk about the connections between Christian healing and traditional western medicine. One thing I taught was the need to bless medications. Many Christians say grace over food. We need to say grace over our medications. I first realized this when I was with my niece, Georgina. When she was ten she was diagnosed with a brain tumor and I was with her at the first dose of chemotherapy. When the two nurses wheeled in the large bag of medication hanging on the shiny metal stand, I watched Georgina. Just for a moment I saw a flash in her eyes. I asked the nurses if we could have five minutes. They very kindly left us. I went to the bag and laid my hands on it and prayed that the medication would hit the target and have no side effects.

I reminded the participants at the conference that the Bible tells us that medications are a gift from God:

> The Lord created medicines out of the earth, and the sensible will not despise them. Was not water made sweet with a tree in order that its power might be known? And he gave skill to human beings that he might be glorified in his marvelous works. By them the physician heals and takes away pain; the pharmacist makes a mixture from them. God's works will never be finished; and from him health spreads over all the earth. (Sirach 38:4–8)

By dispensing accurate doses of the right medications, the pharmacist heals and takes away pain. They are a gift from God.

Four things happen, I believe, when we pray over medications:

1. Prayer changes our perception from denial to the knowledge that the medications are needed. I have observed that some people who are on medications,

especially for emotional or mental issues, find that they feel fine after a few days or weeks and then, by self-diagnosis, decide to come off the prescription or reduce the dosage. The patient may not realize when the symptoms return, though others notice all is not well.

2. Prayer breaks down the barrier of anger and fear about the diagnosis by acknowledging that help is here, from God.

3. Prayer creates a new relationship with the medication when we pray that it will hit the target and have no side effects. We see that the medication is on the side of the patient and is not the enemy—though it is the enemy of the disease!

4. Prayer helps fill the gap between the patient and the prescription itself, allowing the patient to accept the need for medication as part of the healing process.

During my address at the conference I also spoke about the role of the physician in healing, and how God uses the hands of doctors and nurses to bring healing. I told them that on our healing team we anoint the hands of those who will be praying, to commission them as hands for healing. After the talk fifteen doctors lined up, Marine-style, at a forty-five-degree angle from me, an arm's length apart, standing to attention. I am used to people lining up after a talk for me to sign my book, but this was different! What were they up to? They thought I would feel more at home, as a former drill instructor. It was very funny. The ringleader, who was obviously quite a character, explained what was going on and then presented his hands, palms up. "Nigel," he said, "you spoke of anointing hands that they would be 'the hands of Christ.' I want to be an ambassador for Christ. Would you anoint my hands, please? I am a GP and would like to boldly pray for my patients." My eyes were popping out of my head, I was so surprised.

After I anointed his hands the second doctor in line presented his hands, saying, "I am a heart surgeon. I remove diseased hearts and replace them with new ones. I witness the miracles of God in my work, and I would like you to anoint my hands, please." By the time I finished with the fifteenth physician I was in tears. I was deeply moved by the passion and faith of these doctors and surgeons. This was a life-changing moment for me as I witnessed true humility through these very gifted men and women.

Pray for your doctors, your nurses, your caregivers, your pharmacists. There will be a whole new relationship between you.

Several years ago God really got my attention when I witnessed three major miracles of healing in the space of three weeks. My prayers came with much more authority after these experiences. I was leading a healing mission at Glennon House at All Saints' Episcopal Church in Winter Park, Florida. (Glennon House is a healing center named after my mentor from Sydney, Canon Jim Glennon.) I was asked to preach, teach, and pray for people. We prayed with a woman with breast cancer. The next day she was going to have the lump removed from her breast. She was very anxious and concerned about the outcome. When the woman called me the next day, she was astonished. "Nigel," she said, "I was lying on the operating table with the needle inserted into my arm ready for the administration of the medications to knock me out. When the surgeon came in to check on me he placed his hand on my breast looking for the lump that was about to be removed. He kept looking. 'I can't find it,' he said. 'Where is it?' He kept looking, but it was gone. I told him that I had had prayer the day before at All Saints', Winter Park. He said, 'Well, it must have worked.' Everyone in the operating room was ecstatic. 'What do I do now?' I asked the surgeon. 'You can go home,' he said. I thanked God with all of my heart, mind, body, and soul."

I then returned to the Oratory in Connecticut and a week later was leading a healing service in Kent, Connecticut. We prayed for a woman with breast cancer, who was having surgery the next day for the removal of the lump and perhaps the lymph nodes. We all prayed and prayed and believed. The following afternoon I had a phone call from her. She was ecstatic, almost unable to tell the story. "What happened?" I asked. Her story was identical to the one I had just heard from the woman from Winter Park. The lump was gone and she was sent home. The surgery team was ecstatic. When the surgeon asked her what she had been doing, she told him that she had been for prayer at the Oratory of the Little Way. The surgeon told her that he is a Catholic and that he believes in the healing ministry of Jesus. He thanked God right there and then for her healing.

Now all this starts to get really interesting. The following week yet another woman presented with a lump in her breast. She was scheduled to see the *same* surgeon. We prayed and we prayed. The next day she went to the hospital for the procedure. She was lying on the table, all ready to go. The needle was inserted, ready for the anesthetic. The surgeon came in to check on the location of the lump. He checked and checked and it was gone. There was no sign of the lump! A nurse standing in the corner with the paperwork for this patient said, "Well now, doctor, what do I do with all of this paperwork?" The surgeon said, "Tear it up, she has been healed." This time the nurses jumped around in joy, and some pulled out their crosses from beneath their scrubs. There was great euphoria in that surgery that morning. "What do I do?" the patient asked. "You can go home," the doctor replied. That third patient was my wife. Oh, how we rejoiced!

The next day the surgeon called me. "Let's do lunch," he said. We had a wonderful time of conversation and prayer as we spoke about the healer, Jesus. We knew just what Paul meant when he wrote, "May the God of hope fill us with all joy and peace in believing through the power of the Holy Spirit" (Romans 15:13).

CHAPTER 6

Healing the Whole Person
The Healing of Memories

The Spirit of the Lord is on me, because he has anointed me to preach good news to the poor. He has sent me to proclaim freedom for the prisoners and recovery of sight for the blind, to release the oppressed, to proclaim the year of the Lord's favor.
(Luke 4:18–19)

The wounds and scar tissue of the past have molded us into who we are. The good news is that Christ came to heal the sick and set the captives free. A major part of the healing ministry involves releasing those who are captive to memories that still have the power to enslave us. Unforgiveness can wreak havoc upon the heart and soul, chaining us to the past. To be able to see what memories have such power over us, to shine the light of Christ upon them, and to expose them for what they are is truly a gift to the soul. Jesus said, "Then you will know the truth, and the truth will set you free" (John 8:32).

Agnes Sanford developed the idea of "inner healing" or "healing the memories." So many people I meet are captive to memories of past incidents that have crippled their minds and control the present, trying to lock out the future. The mind is in prison! The goal of inner healing, therefore, is to unpack the memories in a safe environment. How is this done?

We must stand on the promise that God will never leave us nor forsake us (Deuteronomy 31:6), even when we endure violence, abuse, or rape. I am often asked the question, "Why God did not prevent the perpetrator from attacking me?" Anger at both the perpetrator and at God often pours out at this point. Many emotions are exposed during inner healing. When we pray for the healing of memories we affirm that Jesus is with us now and is able to do something with those dreadful memories. Just as he witnessed the crime, he is now witnessing the healing as the truth is proclaimed and the memory healed.

Inner healing is rather like taking the memory that is stored on a computer disk out of the brain, allowing Christ to lay his hands on it and heal the memory, and then returning it to the brain, healed. The memory of this part of your life is not erased, but when that memory is triggered the physical reaction and inner torment has gone.

Often people who are captive to their memories feel like prisoners; they are still oppressed by the perpetrator and the crime set upon them. I am amazed daily at this form of prayer, watching God set people free from past hurts and abuse. Inner healing can be the key to setting us free, allowing God to release us from the prison of the past as we come to the realization that the sin and the perpetrator have no power over us any more. As Jesus said, "It is finished."

❋

Many military personnel visit this healing ministry for prayer, and after 9/11 the number shot up. One United States Marine, a sergeant who was trained as a sniper, came for prayer after being medically returned to the States from Iraq. Luckily, I had the afternoon free to work with and pray for this man, who kept calling me "Sir." "My name is Nigel. Please feel free to call me Nigel!" I told him. "Yes sir," came the reply. The sergeant confided in me that he was suffering from post-traumatic stress disorder from his wartime experiences. "How may I pray for you?" I asked. He gave me his history. He was a sniper, and every time he closed his eyes he would vividly see the people he had shot through his sniper scope. "Sir, it is like a slide show, each incident shown in order and very graphic. I do not want to close my eyes, let alone sleep. I just cannot get away from the war!" The images of death were seared onto his dominant eye. The center of a sniper scope is now a circle (in days gone by it was a cross!). Where the lines meet is where the round lands, and this is all magnified by the telescopic effect of the sniper scope, sometimes upside-down. I listened to his story and then we prayed for the healing of memories of his "slide show" thoughts. We spent a long time working on healing these memories through prayer. Many breakthroughs happened as these images were unpacked and given to the Lord. I was astonished at how many "confirmed hits" this young man had had.

Sometimes as we draw near to the end of a session a "door-knobber" happens. The prayers have been offered and then as I stand to say goodbye and have my hand on the doorknob, the supplicant tells me the real reason for the visit. "Sir, I have a need for physical healing as well," the sergeant explained. He then proceeded to tell me a story that truly had me hanging from the rafters.

"Sir, I was involved in a firefight against the Iraqis, entrenched and concealed as a sniper. I was fighting alongside K Company, 42 Commando Royal Marines." My eyes just about popped out of my head. "That was my old unit. I was in K Company, 42 Commando for three years," I explained. The sergeant continued his story. "Two Royal Marines were lying in no-man's land, screaming in pain. One had his right leg below the knee destroyed by an Iraqi .50 cal round and the other had his right shoulder shot away. I compromised my position, Sir."

While under fire, this young man then put one Royal Marine over his shoulder and the other on his hip and ran to the safe zone and eventually to an awaiting MEDEVAC helicopter to be flown to the MASH unit. Luckily, the helicopter medic dragged this sergeant into the chopper too, not wanting to waste time. The sergeant knew that he needed to get back to the firefight, but by this time the medic had a firm hold on his battlefield yoke and would not let go as he physically moved his body into the helicopter. The sergeant sat on the designated seat, snapped the seatbelt clip closed, and took a deep breath. He felt something warm on his back and put his hand up behind his flak jacket. He pulled it out and found it was covered in blood. The medic immediately responded and discovered the man had been shot in the back. There was an entry wound behind the heart and no exit wound; the round had lodged in his heart. The sergeant told me that he was flown to Germany and then returned for medical leave in the USA with an Iraqi bullet in his heart, as it was deemed too dangerous to try to remove it.

It was clear this sergeant had deep faith in the Lord. The Spirit of the sovereign Lord was clearly upon this man, as he embarked on the journey of healing with Christ the healer as his primary focus. There are so many wounds from war, apart from the obvious physical issues. Sometimes the rounds that hit soldiers are not made of steel. The other wounds do not get a dressing and often others cannot see them, but they include deep scar tissue that in time can be healed by God.

A few months after 9/11 I was asked to pray for a former sergeant of the Artillery from the British Army. He had served in World War II and was quite deaf because of the artillery noise of war. This man had been a "FOO" (Forward Observation Officer) and directed artillery fire from an observation post between the guns and the target. His job was to bracket; that is, to radio the artillery position and to say up, down, left, or right a click in order to bring the rounds to the target. This man had managed to keep his wartime thoughts contained for years until the 9/11 headlines came out.

It was the "three thousand killed" that pushed him over the edge. He had managed to keep to himself the fact that he most likely had killed three thousand people in directing artillery fire into villages and enemy locations. The current news created flashbacks for this gentleman and squeezed his mind into the flight/fight mode. He was so traumatized by 9/11 he started exhibiting signs of delayed post-traumatic stress disorder.

We chatted for a very long time and we prayed the healing of memories prayer. When he left the prayer room I made a point of thanking him for serving his country and reminding him that if he had not, I most likely would not be alive. The mind is an amazing thing: here was a case where the memories from many years ago were so powerful they could cause shellshock (or battle fatigue, as it was called in World War II days) almost fifty years later. His memories of those horrific events are still there, but with Christ and through Christ the memories are healed. Through prayer this courageous man was able to affirm Paul's words to the church in Rome:

> Therefore, there is now no condemnation for those who are in Christ Jesus, because through Christ Jesus the law of the Spirit of life set me free from the law of sin and death. (Romans 8:1–2)

Nancy was different. She had had a very tough life with not much love, suffering rejection all of her life in quite nasty ways. Over a period of three years Nancy came to see me every month to have a chat. She would tell me "her story" every time she came, reciting it as if she was reading. It took exactly twenty minutes. I could probably recite it verbatim even now. She had no eye contact during this ritual and almost went somewhere else. I would take a section of her life and unpack it and pray about it, like holding up a single facet of this very rough diamond and letting her see the light of Christ shine on her and those memories. Nancy was hard of hearing and had an over-whelming fear of going blind. Nancy had a bit of a problem with transference, as she wanted to marry me (she was eighty-two and I was forty-four!) and would always ask me to sit next to her. She had a spark in her eye... the salt of the earth.

After two years of monthly chats and work in the area of healing memories and inner healing, she had quite a list of those she needed to forgive. I had an idea. The healing center was very near the Housatonic River. I decided to buy a toy boat, write the names of all those who had caused pain in Nancy's life, put the list on the boat, and launch it down the river. I had forgotten about the plan for a year and then, while I was in a shop, I saw a white hulled toy boat; perfect. I bought the boat and the next time I saw Nancy I produced it. We spent some time writing all the names of those who had caused her pain. So much pain, so many names; what a sad life this woman had led. I then put her in my car and drove the mile or so to the Housatonic River. We said a prayer and I stooped down to release the boat with all the names of those who had been so nasty to Nancy. Nancy danced with joy. "It is finished!" she said. She was so happy. Finally she was able to let go, to give up all that nastiness to God. She was finally able to forgive those who had trespassed against her. What a joyful moment that was. She had the biggest smile on her face that I had ever seen. Her relief was so obvious. She was finally content. What a peaceful mile drive back to the Oratory.

At ten o'clock the next day I had a phone call from her pastor. "Nigel, Nancy died last night. She was found dead in her bed this morning." I wept—oh, did I weep. When I could finally speak again we talked of her life. "Would you be so kind as to preach at her funeral, Nigel?" the pastor asked. I wore a black cassock as I told Nancy's story from the pulpit at her funeral. There were only a handful of people there. No family, just a few of the faithful from the congregation. It was all very sad. When I finished my homily, I was in tears, as were the people who had gathered. Then I took off my cassock to reveal my kilt, picked up my bagpipes that were hidden behind the pulpit, and played "Amazing Grace" for Nancy's soul. It is very hard to play the pipes while crying!

Nancy "got it" in the last twenty-four hours of her life. She had in effect proclaimed what the Lord did on the cross, "Father, forgive them, they do not know what they are doing" (Luke 23:34). In death do we perhaps find the ultimate healing? May the Lord bless your soul, Nancy.

We all have the key to unpack the wounds of life. I was once at St. Andrew's, Chorleywood, London, where my sister Julie had finished a healing mission that I was attending. My sister and I were praying with people and I was led at the very end to go over to someone who was quietly sitting in the front pew. I strongly felt that I should say to the woman, "You have the key." I fought this strange feeling for a while but then slowly walked over to the woman and said, "You have the key." I then walked away, feeling a little weird, like I was some sort of 007 agent.

The woman came over to me and asked for some clarification. I did not have any, except that I had been led to say, "You have the key." Tears started falling down her cheeks. "What is it?" I asked. She then told me that for the past six months she had not left her house. She had been diagnosed with agoraphobia—fear of open spaces. Her house had become like a prison, but she had refused to leave. That night somehow she had been able to come to hear my sister speak at the persuasion of a friend. At the very end of the evening, when she was about to give up, a strange man walks up to her and says, "You have the key"! She had been locked in her house for six months and four words released her. She realized that she had the key literally to unlock the door of her apartment. She knew she also had the key to the kingdom of God, which includes freedom. This captive had been set free. The Lord knew her condition and let her know that he knew. He set her free with the key that was already in her hand.

God works in strange and wonderful ways, as he did in this story of an amazing insight into forgiveness and reconciliation.

It was an ordinary day when Jane showed up for her appointment. Jane is a Messianic Jew who has come to know the Lord. She shared her background with me; she was from Russia and had lost all her family in the Holocaust. She was the sole survivor—or, as she put it, the "soul survivor." She had come to New York by boat and found work, creating a new life for herself in this country.

She told me that she was now a volunteer working with the homeless in the city, teaching art to the misplaced and lonely. She had created quite a ministry and often shared her new faith with those lost souls. After some time she befriended a young man whom she thought she could help. She even trusted him to live in her New York City apartment, sleeping on the couch. This man found a job and started integrating with society. Jane, a very compassionate and caring woman, had picked this man up and given him new life. Jane had lived the story of the Good Samaritan: she had brought him home, bandaged his emotional wounds, and given him a fresh start. The world needs more kind and generous people like Jane.

Listening to Jane's story, I felt that I was waiting for the "other shoe to drop." And then it did. Jane told me that one Saturday morning she took this man to breakfast at a café with tables on the sidewalk. There, the sun was shining and all was quite idyllic, when the relationship hit the wall. Some Hasidic Jews walked by their table. With extreme loathing, the young man then made very nasty and hateful comments about Jewish people. He did not speak loud enough for the passersby to hear, but just assumed that Jane would agree with him.

Jane was furious with this young man. As she sat trembling in outrage, her fists clenched and her teeth clamped, trying not to make a scene in a very public place, the young man had no idea what damage he had done to the relationship. When she was able to calm down, Jane shared her story with this man. He had no idea she was Jewish. He had no idea that she had lost her entire family because of their faith. He sat there white and drained as he understood the gravity of the situation. He then quietly told his story.

"Jane," he said, "I grew up in Argentina, but my parents are German. They fled Germany at the end of World War II to try to save their own lives. Jane, my parents were Nazis!" It was as if time stood still, as if even the noise and the traffic stopped in the city. Jane had a flood of emotions as she realized she had taken the son of Nazis into her house. The question, "Did his parents murder my family?" kept going through her mind. "How can I sleep tonight," she thought, "knowing that the son of Nazis is sleeping in my living room?" Jane was shaking again. She had two options: she could kick him out onto the street, or pray through the situation. She boldly chose the latter.

She and I prayed through the situation, with Jane allowing God to help her forgive. Slowly she and the young man worked out their past history and chose to become even deeper friends as God "cleaned up" the mess. Eventually the young man was able to move out and live in the community. A restored homeless man taken in by a truly incredible woman, who certainly knows the Lord.

※

While it can take months or even years for the whole person to be healed of powerful memories, here is a story that shows how inner healing can also take place spontaneously, in the blink of an eye.

Recently the Lord healed me of a very nasty memory that had been lurking in my mind since 1972. It had been an unhealed wound for thirty-five years, and I had a bad case of unforgiveness lodged in my mind. A few months ago I was the keynote speaker for a meeting of the Association of Christian Therapists held at the Espousal Retreat House and Conference Center in Waltham, Massachusetts. A slightly daunting task, I must say: forty-nine mostly Roman Catholic therapists, coming to learn more about the healing grace of Jesus. On the third day I was sitting at the lunch table with Fr. Larry Carew, a Catholic priest who is a dear friend and mentor. Suddenly a painful old memory came to mind. I was in Belfast again; it was 1972. My friend Tim had just been shot. I was actually looking at him, waiting on his command, when I heard a loud BANG and down he went. I will always remember his scream of pain as he yelped into his radio, "ARGH, I've been hit!"

Young teens began dancing and kicking his blood around, shouting in joy, "Another f#$%&*!# British solider has been shot!"

"Hey, that is my friend's blood you're kicking around!" I wanted to shout, but I could not do anything as I was lying in cover awaiting the next bullet—perhaps for me! What will it feel like? I wondered. How will I cope with the pain? What is it like to die? I was so angry at those kids; I had a rifle in my hands. . . .

That memory had haunted me for thirty-five years. But as I sat next to my Catholic friend and mentor, it happened. A deep inner healing, in the blink of an eye. Vividly, I saw in my mind Jesus standing in Tim's blood, arms outstretched, looking intensely at me across the street as if to say, "Nigel, these are my kids. Suffer the little children to come unto me. Forgive them, they know not what they are doing." Then, in this godly reframing of a memory, I saw Jesus looking down at those celebrating teens and heard him say to them, "This is *my* blood. Tim was made in my image. He is my kid, too. Please don't kick my blood around."

My jaw dropped as the chains of that memory simply fell away from me. The deep wound was spontaneously healed. I knew Jesus was standing in the gap, bringing the power of reconciliation. God is so good. I am a very different person now; the shadow of death and the pain of unforgiveness has gone. They left me in a nanosecond, with the vision of Christ standing in my friend's blood. Glory to God, whose power working in us is able to do far more that we can possibly imagine.

CHAPTER 7

Fresh from Heaven
Praying with Children

At that time Jesus, full of joy through the Holy Spirit, said, "I praise you, Father, Lord of heaven and earth, because you have hidden these things from the wise and learned, and revealed them to little children." (Luke 10:21)

I once heard a poignant story of a little girl who had just received a new brother. She kept nagging her parents to have a private word with her brother. Finally the parents gave in and let their daughter go into her brother's room alone, while they listened on the baby monitor in the room. The girl asked her brother, "Please remind me what God is like. I am beginning to forget." It was as if the girl knew that her brother was closer to God, a freshly delivered soul from heaven.

"Jesus, full of joy through the Holy Spirit." What a beautiful image. How often are we filled with that joy, that love, and that compassion? Perhaps children are more often filled with that joy because they are closer to the life of the spirit. Praying with children—and animals, for that matter—is often much easier than praying with adults. Children have an innocence, an open desire, a willingness to be prayed with and for, while many adults have built walls of protection around themselves. The trusting look of a baby can be so beautiful, seeing not only my face but somehow clear into the soul.

Praying with children can be very emotional for the prayer team, especially if the child has been enduring painful medical treatments. The look in a child's eyes when the prayer team comes to pray can be heartbreaking; it is as if the child is asking, "Have you come to stick another needle in me or can you really help me without hurting me?" Yet the good news is that often children will receive prayer much more willingly than adults and will enter into the prayer with a conviction that is refreshing and indeed faith-building for the rest of us. They have not had time to accumulate as much baggage as adults, and in most cases one can get on with the prayer with much less time and effort. Those who are praying can really zero into the issue and pray with gentle compassion right into the target of the disease or sickness. I have so often seen a child's wide-eyed look of trust and fear and helplessness and sorrow that it is etched into my mind; I have felt the pain of these children sear my heart. The look that says, "Please, I need help," can be a powerful stimulant to pray truly from the heart, focusing on the need with compassion, faith, and love. All the peripheral issues move to the edge and the main concern is consumed with loving, heartfelt prayer, the very love of God pouring into those cells that need to be put right.

When praying for a baby, the history of the disease is gathered from the parents or other adults, and a gentle prayer is offered as hands are laid on the baby. Not too many hands, as that can be quite frightening for an infant. A gentle, calm, and peaceful environment is needed as the disease is washed with prayer. I sometimes have the image of a funnel filled with all the prayers of the parents, friends, and churches. The spout of the funnel is placed on the diseased area, so that a concentrated, targeted, and voluminous mass of prayer fills the area with the presence of Jesus himself. Often the child will fall asleep during or after the prayer; such is the presence of peace. Toddlers and some older children can be agitated; ideally the child would be still and receptive, but that does not always happen. That's fine, since even a quick touch can help. Just being in the presence of the Lord is healing; just showing up with a little faith is all that is needed sometimes.

When praying for infants and children do not neglect the parents and those in the background. It is good to anoint their hands and to pray for them, too. Lay a hand on their back, over the heart, and pray for peace and wisdom. Come alongside them with prayer. "Carry each other's burdens, and in this way you will fulfill the law of Christ" (Galatians 6:2).

When it comes to adolescents, I often remember the axiom, "You can lead a horse to water but you cannot make him drink." You can, however, make him thirsty! When I am working with a crowd of teens I often find there is a certain pulling back to begin with, usually because of peer pressure and the need to "be cool." The first minute or two can be a little tense as they are sizing up the situation. Asking a question like "Who is here on your own free will and who has been dragged here by your parents?" is a good ice-breaker. The "dragged" often sit at the back and are huddled in safety within the pack, but at least they are there; so often the presence of God simply rubs off on them and they are drawn in.

When teens hear the message of the healing power of Jesus, the Holy Spirit takes over and a genuine thirst becomes visible. Telling the story is what is needed—the story of the gospel, the stories of healing, the stories of life. I have found that no matter what our age, people enjoy stories. In listening to stories we have a sense of belonging, of being drawn into the love of a caring parent who tells us stories at that special time of going to bed. Jesus himself told the truth of the kingdom of God in stories!

I do find it quite exhilarating to watch God at work with this age group. Teens need to be loved, and Jesus loves them. It is such a wonderful thing to watch the "Aha" moment transform young lives. I have witnessed teens melt when they realize that you are on their side, and that Jesus truly loves them. At first they may sit with their arms folded in a defiant stance of disinterested boredom, but as they become open to the message of God's healing grace their bodies show their total acceptance.

Their willingness to pray for one another once the lines of communication have been opened and the "teen wall" has been broken is amazing. I often teach them how to pray with each other in groups of three or four and then stand back to see the emotion of love pour out into the hearts of so many. The tears and the laughter they share are a most wonderful thing to behold, and the love and compassion teens are capable of is palpable. I will always remember the smile of a particular young woman, teeth covered in braces, who was so enthusiastic for the Lord and who thanked God and me so passionately. The questions and the smiles afterward warm my soul, when the initial aloofness is broken down in the realization that God loves them, too. I know how it feels—it was a sixteen-year-old who brought me to Jesus at 3 P.M. on March 10, 1972!

I have met so many children and even more adults who did not have the privilege of knowing they are loved, whose parents did a very good job in rejecting the child. That wall of rejection can be almost insurmountable in youths and adults who have not received that parental love. The image of God sometimes needs to be healed if the image of the earthly parent is abusive or neglectful.

If you are new to the healing ministry, I encourage you to try praying with a child with a minor problem, like a headache. Ask permission to lay your hands on their head and with an open mind and heart, either out loud or in your mind quietly ask the Lord to take away the pain. Do not ask God to give you the pain; we do not need to do that, as the Lord Jesus took that pain to the cross. Spend a little time in faith praying for the child and "take on to believe" that God is opening the blood vessels that have been restricted to release the pain. When you have finished allow time for a little peace and then quietly ask the child, "How do you feel?" You may be pleasantly surprised!

In 1998 the parents of a seven-year-old girl with Wolff-Parkinson-White Syndrome, a heart condition that is like a short-circuit in the heart's electrical system, came to me to ask for prayer. April's heart rate would unexpectedly go into double time, suddenly switching to about two hundred beats per minute, and attempts to control it through medication had failed. Sometimes she would be sitting quietly on the couch when she would put a hand to her chest and say, "Mom, I'm having an episode." I had prayed for April before, when she was only four years old: her first cardiac ablation had ended in a one-in-ten-thousand complication, and in the aftermath I had prayed for April, that she might be healed, that God would protect her, that her faith and belief in his power and love would continue and strengthen. Three years later, it was time for another cardiac ablation. As the family prepared for the three-thousand-mile trip across the United States to see the doctor who was one of the pioneers of the procedure, they asked me to pray once again for their daughter.

When I arrived at their home, April's mother, Sandra Buscher, told me that April was feeling sad because Woolly, her pet caterpillar, had died. "It went into its cocoon and came out as a tiger moth," Sandra said, "but now it is dead. Woolly hasn't moved for three days." I asked April about Woolly, and she led me into an adjoining room to Woolly's container. She told me stories about how special Woolly was to her, how she found the black and brown woolly bear caterpillar on their driveway, how it used to walk around and around the edge of the bottle cap they used as its water dish, how it would hang its head over the edge of the bottle cap and roll its face around in the water. Woolly loved the color red, and would climb quickly from April's hand to her red sweatshirt when she was wearing it. In late autumn they put a piece of red fabric in Woolly's cage and he spun his cocoon on the fabric that night. By chance April had looked into his container just as Woolly was emerging from his cocoon, but she had never seen him fly. That was a big part of her sadness. Woolly had seemed so happy as a caterpillar, but after he turned to a moth she had never seen him fly. For three days now, April told me, Woolly had laid still and lifeless on the bottom of his cage.

I asked April if she would like to pray with me for Woolly. We thanked God for the joy Woolly had brought to her, and asked God to watch over Woolly and heal him if possible. After the prayer April looked in astonishment at Woolly. The antennae started moving, the legs started moving, the wings heaved, and Woolly flipped over and flew to the window.

After that we had a brief conversation about April's upcoming medical procedure and I prayed for her, for her family, and for the doctors who would perform the cardiac ablation. That night, Sandra reports, she discovered Woolly was flying around his container! "April, come here!" she called. "There's something you need to see...." They watched Woolly fly each night for a few days before releasing him outdoors, praying that God would watch over Woolly and again thanking God for the joy Woolly had brought to April.

Sandra continues the story in her own words:

As we traveled to California for April's procedure, I wondered about the miracle of Woolly. Had he really been dead prior to Nigel's prayers? Or had we just never looked at the right time of day to see him fly prior to the prayers? Whatever the answer, it did not diminish the miracle for me. Nigel and April had prayed for Woolly, believing him to be dead, and knowing April's greatest sadness was that she had never seen Woolly fly once he became a moth. That very day after praying with Nigel, April got to see Woolly fly.

God is kind and wise in ways we can't always imagine. As we left on our trip, I thought the experience with Woolly was reassuring for my little girl and that God was kind to send us off with some reassurance that he was close by and aware of our concerns no matter how seemingly small they were. I didn't know how much I, myself, would draw on the experience to carry me through my daughter's operation.

The night before we arrived in San Diego, our fear was palpable in the air of our hotel room. So I started talking about our experiences with faith to reassure my children—and myself. Woolly stood out as a reminder that God listens when we pray and that he can accomplish things we can't even imagine.

The next day's travel went smoothly, and we got safely settled in our hotel room. The following day we went to the hospital for a pre-op visit with the doctor. He walked us through the different areas of the hospital to show us where April would be the next day, where we would wait for her. One of the last things my husband and I talked about with the doctor was anesthesia. As we stood in an empty corridor outside the procedure room, the doctor told us they would take April so low with the anesthesia that her heart would stop. Once her heart stopped, the doctor would cauterize a small section of her heart tissue. Then they would bring her back up from the depths of the anesthesia so her heart would start beating again. All of this would take place in a matter of seconds. For a moment I was speechless. In the previous procedure April had been heavily sedated, but not under general anesthesia. Now this doctor was going to stop April's heart!

My shock must have shown on my face, because the doctor quickly reassured me that this was how he does all of his procedures, always with the same anesthesiologist so they are both very experienced. He explained that he needed to stop April's heart to make sure the energy delivered to cauterize the heart tissue went to the right place. I realized that I just had to accept this, even though I couldn't comprehend it emotionally. I had to find a way to cope with my fear. I knew my children were taking cues from me and I didn't want them to be afraid.

So I thought of Woolly. To all outward appearances, Woolly had been dead—whether he was in deep hibernation during daylight hours, or whether he was truly dead, he had given no indication of life. So it would be with April. Her body systems would be lowered with the anesthesia until her heart stopped, and she would come back to life just as Woolly had. It was then I appreciated the full gift of our experience with Nigel. God was kind and wise to give us an experience with faith that would carry me through my darkest hour, so I in turn could help carry my family.

April's procedure was successful the next day. She knew it as soon as she awoke from the anesthesia. She could feel the difference with every beat of her heart. Had I just witnessed death being transformed into resurrection twice, both with Woolly and now with my daughter April?

We have carried that experience of faith with us, in good times and in bad. We believe the miracles that come into our lives aren't just for one day, but are meant to sustain us and to help others believe that miracles are possible. Our family has been blessed, time and again, with miracles large and small. We have also been challenged in many ways, and my daughter continues to have medical difficulties even though her heart's electrical problem was resolved that day. But with God, who is kind and wise in ways we cannot always imagine, we face each day with gratitude and hope.

CHAPTER 8

When Healing Doesn't Happen

Blocks to God's Healing Grace

Jesus could not do any miracles there, except lay his hands on a few sick people and heal them. And he was amazed at their lack of faith. (Mark 6:5–6)

There are so many blocks to being healed. We build walls around ourselves that block the love of God. Sometimes the walls are there for self-defense; sometimes they are the result of holding on to past injuries or unbelief or bad choices. Over the years of praying for people I have encountered several major blocks to healing: unforgiveness, inner vows, unworthiness, occult involvement, and a negative approach. There are others of course, but most blocks to healing will fall into one of these general categories.

Unforgiveness
The number one block to being healed that I see when praying for people is unforgiveness. So many people carry the "cancer of unforgiveness" in their hearts, giving power to the one who caused the injury even when the perpetrator is long gone. The sin of the past still wounds us when we do not forgive. "But why should I forgive when he has caused so much pain in my life?" I am so often asked. This is a valid question; the refusal to forgive can be justified in so many ways. Forgiveness is not easy.

When praying for someone for healing it is important to remember that forgiveness is a process. There are stages of forgiveness, and in many cases we will need to encourage people to take small steps toward the goal of total forgiveness. If they cannot yet honestly and truly forgive the perpetrator, can they allow God to help them take the first step? Can they say, "Here I am, God. You know I cannot do this yet but would you be so kind as to forgive this person for me until I can come to a place of forgiveness, until I can finally let this situation go? I hand it all over to you, Lord." Only when the person is ready should he or she be encouraged to say to the person who caused the hurt, "Will you forgive me for the anger and rage I have had against you for the pain you have caused me?" This can be done if the person is alive and present, or not. It is best to speak this with another person listening, or to write it down in the form of a letter that is most often not sent. What happens is that the situation is turned around: the power that held the person captive to the pain and sin of the past is released once and for all.

The Bible tells us that forgiveness is not an option: we must forgive if we are to be forgiven and healed: "For if you forgive men when they sin against you, your heavenly Father will also forgive you. But if you do not forgive men their sins, your Father will not forgive your sins" (Matthew 6:14–15). Now *that* is quite clear! God gave us free will to love one another and to hurt one another. If we can truly let go of the power of sin that holds sway over us, our lives can be changed.

I well remember praying with someone whose healing had been blocked by unforgiveness. Robert had had surgery on his knee nine months before and it was not getting better; in fact, after several visits to the doctor it had grown worse! The wound was just not healing and it was causing this man extreme pain. He did not live too far away and I was able to go to his home and visit him. In the English way he gave me a cup of tea, and we chatted at length about the history of his knee. Since I knew that unforgiveness can be a powerful block to healing, at some point I asked him, "Do you need to forgive anyone?" In this case I think we got to the root cause very quickly. "There is someone of whom I need to ask forgiveness," Robert affirmed. He went on to tell me something that had happened ten years earlier. He had upset his sister-in-law and they had not spoken or seen each other since. He had actually avoided family gatherings so he would not need to be confronted with this woman. We unpacked the story and then I prayed for the knee and for reconciliation of these two related by marriage. I left trusting that God would take care of the situation, by faith.

Three days later I received a very excited phone call from this neighbor. "Nigel," he proclaimed, "my knee is fine. It has healed and you can barely see the scar tissue! There is no pain and I am walking with no problems. My doctor is amazed. Thanks be to God!" He went on to tell me that as soon as I walked out of the door of his house he said a prayer and immediately picked up the phone to call his sister-in-law. He told me that her startled response to the call was, "I have been waiting for this call for ten years."

The baggage was unpacked, Robert said he was sorry for the pain and misunderstanding he had caused, forgiveness was granted, and God healed him—all in quick succession! Amen, thanks be to God for the fruit of answered prayer. Robert confessed and his knee was allowed to bend toward God in thanksgiving.

It is truly amazing the baggage we all carry, especially the skeletons in the closet that are so often shrouded in unforgiveness. Recently I was praying with someone in regard to the "skeleton in the closet" and it was as if the skeleton said to me, "Hey Nigel, thanks for opening the door. I have been locked in here way too long. I am out of here!" The skeleton got up and ran away. That skeleton no longer had any power. The supplicant and I laughed and laughed—laughter is so healing.

Inner Vows

An inner vow is a promise we make to ourselves after we endure a painful incident or experience in life, such as rejection or rape or divorce or betrayal. We vow, "I will never trust a man again" or "I will never talk to my mother-in-law again," and so on. We make promises to ourselves that bind our actions for years to come and prevent the healing power of God from operating in our lives. It is vitally important to expose these inner vows that are controlling one's life. I have seen so many people set free after uncovering these private and personal inner vows in the safe and loving presence of the prayer team. Sometimes these vows are not easy to let go. Perhaps it has been years since the incident took place, and in the meantime the brain has gotten into a habitual way of thinking about the experience and the effect it had on our lives. When we give ourselves permission to be set free from these vows, life can take on new meaning as once and for all God takes away the pain and suffering that has gone on for so long.

Unworthiness

Another major block to being healed is a sense of unworthiness, of not being important or good enough to receive

God's attention and loving care. It is as if someone says, "I am not worthy to be healed; there are so many others out there who need God's healing more than I." I hear this over and over again. It breaks my heart. God gave his only Son that we might have life and have it abundantly! God wants us to live a full life even in this Garden of Eden that we have so messed up. "I am the LORD who heals you" (Exodus 15:26).

How worthy was the demoniac, the blind man, the leper? And yet Jesus healed them all. We are made worthy through the fact that God sent his only Son that we might live. If unworthiness is an issue with you, if low self-esteem is a concern, give it to God. Release your clenched fists and hand it all over to God. Then stand back and see what happens. You may have to do this over and over, but keep doing it. When our sense of unworthiness is handed over to God, our hearts, minds, and bodies are freed to accept the healing God wants to give us.

Occult Involvement

I am truly amazed at the number of times I see the effect of involvement in the occult when someone comes to pray for healing. Sometimes the involvement was long ago and seemingly rather innocent; often the entry portal for the occult can be traced back to playing with a Ouija board or other such "game." Some people have even been the source or recipient of curses, and need to be released from them. If you have been involved in anything to do with the occult, it is time to let that go, since it is vital that any power over you that is not from God be severed. You might need to seek reconciliation with God in a formal confession with a clergyperson, so that you may be free. Jesus came to set the captives free, and he gave to his apostles power and authority to bind the evil spirits who oppressed his people: "He called his twelve disciples to him and gave them authority to drive out evil spirits and to cure every kind of disease and sickness" (Matthew 10:1).

Some time ago I was invited to lead a healing service at a religious institution that I discovered had rented their facility to a group who practiced Wicka. I do not think that the person responsible for community relations realized the implications of that decision, or even knew what Wicka is. Thank God I knew this before the service. The prayer team was prayed up, I was ready (I thought!), and the opening hymn was announced. The chapel felt cold, though, and somehow something was very wrong. I began the prayers and realized that the worship was "flat-lining"; nothing was happening. I prayed and pleaded, but to no avail. It was as if we were not supposed to be there. Where are you, God? What should I do? You said that you would never leave me or forsake me; what is going on? It felt so lonely trying to lead this particular time of worship. I strongly felt that our prayer was going nowhere.

I was in a rector's office once and saw a sign on his desk that said, "Godisnowhere." I read it twice and without hesitating asked the rector why a man of God would have a sign that clearly stated that "God is nowhere." "Have you lost your faith, man?" I asked. He smiled a knowing smile. "Read it again, Nigel," he said. I did and then I saw it: "God is nowhere" becomes "God is now here" when you move the *w*. For the first ten or fifteen minutes of this healing service I was experiencing "God is nowhere," but I was about to see that "God is now here."

I prayed again and felt that I was going to have to send everyone home. I had made up my mind that the Holy Spirit was not going to show up because of the previous weekend's shenanigans. I walked slowly with a low head and stood at the crossing of the large chapel. I took a breath, ready to tell people to go home. As I opened my mouth to speak, I noticed a raised hand in the back pew and I heard myself saying, "Yes, madam, what would you like to share?"

The woman said, "Nigel, do you remember me?" I responded in the negative. She announced to the gathered community that she had brought a friend to my house ten years ago so that I could pray with her; to affirm the truth of her story she went on to describe my living room in great detail. Her friend was scheduled for surgery the next day to remove a cancerous growth in her brain. The woman continued: "It was a Sunday after church. You sat her down, you anointed my hands that I might pray, and you anointed my friend's head. You prayed very specifically that the brain tumor would turn to liquid. Nigel, you were very adamant."

She went on, "The next day, Monday, was a very interesting day. I went with my friend and her parents to the hospital and waited in the waiting room for news of the completed operation. We were told that the wait would be several hours. In what seemed like a very short time the surgeon came to give us the news. We were worried, as it seemed too soon. But the surgeon smiled and told her parents that their daughter would be fine, that he was able to remove all the tumor. Then he added, 'By the way, this was a very strange surgery. After the site was opened I found out that the mass was liquid and did not correspond with the MRI. I have never seen anything like it.'" This young woman was now crying. I also had tears in my eyes at this point, and when I looked around at the congregation I could see that many jaws had dropped in astonishment. Here we were ten years later and this was the first news I had heard of the answered prayer of this miracle.

After the woman finished speaking, the Spirit of the Sovereign Lord showed up with power. The chapel was immediately filled with love and God's presence, as if it was indeed filled with the Holy Spirit, who like a rush of wind pushed out whatever had happened there before us. Suddenly, spontaneous worship burst forth. What a joy, what a relief. The fruit of that service was amazing, to say the least. No one had any idea how close I had been to packing this healing service up and going home.

I laid hands on many people that night and was praying over a young man when a word came to me. I asked him if he had been baptized and he responded, "No, but I have been thinking about it. My grandfather has been trying to lead me to baptism but I just have not made the commitment yet. How did you know?" My mind was racing. "I am a lay person, and I can do an emergency baptism," I heard myself saying excitedly. He looked at me and smiled. "Actually, my pastor is here. Perhaps we can ask him." I went to his pastor and said that I had been praying with one of his parishioners and felt that he was seeking Holy Baptism, and asked if he would baptize him. He said, "Let's do it right now."

Immediately the healing service took on a whole new life, abundant life. The congregation gathered around this man and his pastor baptized him right there and then. I just stood there with tears falling down my cheeks. The joy and celebration was amazing as so many denominations gathered to witness a healing in the form of baptism.

My journey back to the Oratory was a long one of pleading forgiveness from God. "I doubted you, Lord. I am so sorry. Lord, I do believe; help me overcome my unbelief." We had witnessed a wonderful miracle that evening. Because I had doubted that God was present among us, and had thought the power of occult involvement was stronger than the power of God, I had nearly sent sixty-five people home. How wrong I was. It was quite a lesson to learn and one that fills my heart to this day.

Negative Attitude

I am sure you can bring people to mind who are negative in a majority of areas in their life. Perhaps you are one of them! Some people cannot see past the negative aspects and possibilities of life; they focus on the sort of despairing thoughts that drag everyone down who comes in contact with them. The "drowning man" syndrome, if you will. We get pulled under the water as we try to help someone else. My mentor for many years, Canon Jim Glennon, would not have eye contact with me if I was being negative. It took me a while to realize what he was doing, but when I did grasp it I realized I had an option in life. I could always focus on the negative and get dragged under, or I could focus on the positive, actively seeking first God's kingdom. I have a choice.

With God's help we can change our thoughts in conversation from the negative to the positive. Our thoughts and attitudes have a tremendous and often overlooked power in our lives. Try this with someone. Stand in front of someone and ask him to put out his strongest arm. Ask him to make a fist and say, "I am strong. I believe. Thank you, Jesus, for your strength in me." As this is being said, put your hand on his fist and push down. See what happens. Then ask the person to shake out his arm. Now have him put out the same arm while saying, "I am weak. I am a nobody. I am nothing." Now again push down on his fist and see what happens. Usually you see how true it is that "we are what we think we are." A change in attitude could be a first and important step toward your healing.

A study in the United Kingdom identified that eighty percent of what we say is negative and twenty percent of what we say is positive. It appears that most humans are ready to say something negative before focusing on the positive. Within the healing community I often teach and remind people of this. When I hear someone focusing only on the negative, I just say "Eighty/twenty." It is a not-so-subtle way of refocusing on the positive. Sometimes we need the help of a friend or a prayer group to help us refocus and to be accountable for our negative thoughts that block us from the healing grace of God. When we choose the negative approach there will not be much fruit to our prayer, if any.

Like most people, I am guilty of this eighty/twenty attitude. One summer I had two seminarian interns, one from Nashotah House in Wisconsin and the other from

Wycliffe Hall, in Oxford, England. On a certain day I saw that two people were coming from Connecticut for ministry. I recognized their names, since I had seen them on many occasions over several years. I shared with the two interns that these two people, who were coming independently, were quite likely to take a bite out of them, and warned them to be careful with these two "short-fused" souls. Like many of the people who come for healing, these two people were filled with anger and resentment and tended to transfer those issues to me or the prayer team. Although I had not seen them for two years, I was ready to be "challenged"!

Halfway through the first prayer session I realized that I had made a huge mistake. In both cases the individuals were so transformed that they made eye contact and were kind to the prayer team, nice to other people, and very pleasant to be with. I felt such a warmth in my chest—they were healed! I had not allowed for the possibility that the seed of the healing grace of Christ that had been planted years before might transform a person. Healing at a much deeper level, the soul. I had to stop the session and confess to the supplicants that I had misjudged them. I told them that I had even warned my interns, who were both present, to be careful of them because of the anger they had shown during their previous visits. I confessed that I had not allowed for the fact that God heals; I had forgotten that God restores and even resurrects people! Hello, Mumford! It was a godly reminder that even souls who are wounded, cowering, and defensive, who are ready to pounce with teeth exposed, who are negatively toxic to be with, can be healed by the pure love of God.

I asked for forgiveness from both supplicants, who both smiled broadly at this revelation. They had both realized that over time God had healed them, and they had actually come simply to say thank you. Their faces were beatific, positively radiant, filled with joy at this healing. I had witnessed and affirmed the change in them, and the interns had witnessed the miracle of God's healing. I had been guilty of the eighty/twenty attitude, but God redeemed the occasion and made it a source of joy for us all.

PART TWO

Sharing in the Ministry of Healing

*The apostles performed many miraculous signs and
wonders among the people. . . . More and more men
and women believed in the Lord and were added
to their number. As a result, people brought the sick
into the streets and laid them on beds and mats so
that at least Peter's shadow might fall on some of
them as he passed by. Crowds gathered also from
the towns around Jerusalem, bringing their sick
and those tormented by evil spirits, and all of them
were healed.*

(Acts 5:12, 14–16)

CHAPTER 9

Listen, Love, and Pray
Healing Ministry Basics

*This is the assurance we have in approaching God:
that if we ask anything according to his will, he
hears us. And if we know that he hears us—whatever we ask—we know that we have what we asked
of him. (1 John 5:14–15)*

Over the course of my experiences with the healing
ministry I have observed ten major ingredients to
healing. There are of course many other factors, but in my
view these are the key issues:

1) Christian healing is about releasing disease in the
name of Jesus Christ.

2) Christian healing is about the love of Christ.

3) When we pray something *always* happens.

4) We need to come to this ministry with an attitude of gratitude: "Give thanks in all things."

5) Not everyone is cured, but everyone is healed.

6) Christian healing is about being an open vessel for the Lord to work through.

7) The healing process is a mystery and we do not need to know the answers to all our questions.

8) Christian healing is about faith, but not necessarily the faith of the supplicant. The faith of those who are praying is sometimes all that is needed.

9) Christian healing is faith working through love, for the love of Jesus Christ is manifested and known through the experience of healing.

10) Health and salvation are the will of God.

Three words express the key to the healing ministry: listen, love, and pray. If you can *really* listen, if you can love in the name of Jesus, and if you can pray, then you have all that is really necessary.

First, *listen.* Listen with all your heart, mind, body, and soul. Listen to what is being said, to what is not being said, and to what the Lord is saying. We usually do not listen well in the course of our everyday lives, and as ministers of God's healing grace we must learn to listen in a holy manner. We must really listen to the issue being presented and unpack it in our minds. Look for the root; ask, what is the cause? People need to be heard. They need to tell their story. Those who are sick are often alienated from the community, even from those closest to them, because of their sickness; those who have been abused know the pain of rejection; those who are poor or weak or lonely are quite often shunned and put aside in our society. It is the call of a minister of healing (lay or ordained) to help override that alienation and abuse in showing the love and compassion of the Christ himself, and the first step in doing that is listening.

Second, *love*. We must love as Christ taught us. Love is essential when praying for healing. Jesus said, "Love the Lord your God with all your heart and with all your soul and with all your mind and with all your strength." And, "Love your neighbor as yourself" (Mark 12:30–31). Sometimes love needs some work, though! If you cannot love the person, ask God to help you to love that person. If you still cannot love the person, take it to your spiritual director and find out what is within you that is blocking that love. What is being triggered in you? What needs to be healed in you?

Finally, *pray*. Pray with everything you have, with all your faith, with all your being. Believe without doubt; pray, "Lord, I do believe; help me overcome my unbelief." Or even just pray, "Lord, I believe." Take on to believe with all you have been given by faith. Have confidence in approaching God in asking and interceding for others and for yourself. Jesus has commanded us to preach the kingdom and heal the sick, and God is listening to every thought and prayer. Take on a humble, holy boldness and a gentle confidence of trust. Put on faith and wear it like an old favorite sweater.

The sculptor Michelangelo would look at a block of Carrera marble and know there was a statue inside. He approached the block with the thought that his job was to cut away the marble that was not needed in order to reveal the perfect sculpture within. Perhaps Jesus looked at those who were sick in the same way, knowing that once their disease and sin and unforgiveness were chipped away, the beautiful, whole person would emerge.

We who share in Christ's healing ministry need to consider how we approach what seems in our mind to be impossible. After all, it *is* impossible—without God. The presenting need can indeed be a block, perhaps a stumbling block. We walk around it, we circle it, we look at it through narrow eyes. We may be intimidated by the cancer, the pain, the arthritis, the ALS, the obsession, the sickness, the diagnosis, the mental disability, the emotional weight, the loss, the generational baggage, the rejection, the abuse—the list goes on and on. We may feel totally inadequate. We may wonder who we think we are, boldly asking God to heal these deep-seated issues of life and death. We need to remember that Jesus only asks us to pray; the rest is up to God. Now what, Lord? Now what do I do?

How to Pray for Healing

> Jesus said to them, "These signs will accompany those who believe:... they will place their hands on sick people, and they will get well." (Mark 16:17–18)

I am a cradle Anglican and have that British reserve! Extroverted television evangelists can push my buttons a little—all that shouting and pushing people over. I have a friend who is also very reserved; once, in order to make a point about how *not* to pray, he asked a very tall man to come forward in front of two hundred people. "This is how we don't pray," he said, as he took a run at him and smacked him on the forehead, shouting, "Be healed in the name of Jesus." The man fell to the floor. Laughter erupted from the crowd. A week later the man wrote to my friend. "Thank you," he said. "I was healed of cancer that day." Well, you never know what God is up to.

How do we go about praying for healing? What do we need to do to receive the healing grace of Jesus? I have found there are seven elements we need to take into consideration:

1) We need to turn to Christ.

2) We need to turn from our sin.

3) We need to forgive and to ask for forgiveness.

4) We need to let go of the blocks to our healing.

5) We need to ask God to heal us.

6) We need to thank God for the healing that is taking place.

7) We need to receive our healing.

Now this list sounds so simple, and in one sense it is. It takes time, though, to learn to tune in to each element as we listen, love, and pray for the people who come for healing, and for ourselves.

Praying for Other People
The first thing to do in praying for others is to check in with ourselves and with God. How should I do this, God? How should I pray? Do I have the faith to pray in hope for what I do not see? If you don't, *ask* for the gift of faith.

After getting certain details about the person (name, marital status, job, faith background, faith/denomination now, children, and so on), I ask, "How may I pray for you?" Ask the person to be very specific, and get the precise details and history of the presenting concern. Listen—and I mean *really* listen—to the supplicant. As you listen to the person's story, spend time on each of the points in the list above, focusing fully on each one, unpacking the baggage. Some will need more attention than others. Pay attention to the details; you need to understand what is the source of the disease or problem, so clarify anything that you are not sure of. Listen to what the supplicant is saying and what he or she is *not* saying. And listen to God.

Love the person as Christ loves us. You have a beloved soul before you, who is sharing a deep woundedness and yearning for wholeness. If you are struggling to have love for this person, ask God to help you see him or her through God's eyes. My friend, this is all about love, and if you can be very gentle, kind, and loving, with no shouting or harsh words, you will be an open vessel for the love and compassion of Jesus.

Then give it all to the Lord. Hand it over. "Here you are, God. This is everything I can think of. I even give you what I do not remember." Having done all that, stand firm on the promise of God to hear us even when we do not have all the words we need. "The Spirit helps us in our weakness. We do not know what we ought to pray, but the Spirit himself intercedes for us with groans that words cannot express. And he who searches our hearts knows the mind of the Spirit, because the Spirit intercedes for the saints in accordance with God's will" (Romans 8:26–27). When you do not know what else to say, let the Spirit pray for the person. Say, "Here, God, you do it. I cannot do this but you can, and I believe that you are doing it now." That is a very simple prayer of faith. Take on to believe.

Now the moment has come to stretch forth your hand in the name of Jesus. It is time to pray. Ask God, "Do you want me to lay hands on this person, Lord?" If so, then always ask supplicants if you may lay your hands on them, even if you prayed for them just yesterday. Abuse often comes from human hands, so be very careful not to retraumatize the supplicant. Keep your hand still when you place it in an area near the concern or upon the head, back, hand, or foot. Do not massage the area or move your hand as you pray. As you touch the person's body, allow the love of Christ's healing touch to go right into the wound and scar tissue.

Then ask, "Do I need words, God?" Try praying in silence to start with. Silence is good! Then, as your confidence grows, ask on behalf of the person with whom you are praying. Do not worry about what you are going to say. Pray the history. All you are doing is praying what you have heard. You are affirming that you have grasped what the person needs and God is hearing what you are saying. As you offer up the person's history to God, pray with accuracy. What do I mean by that? Pray as if you have a scalpel in your hand and go right into the issue. In other words, cut the cancer out! Cut out the unforgiveness, cut out the disease, cut out the lack of faith, cut out the negativity, cut out what is not of the Lord. Pray with love, pray with no condemnation or judgment. Pray with faith.

As you pray, avoid the pitfall of comparing "your woes" with those of the supplicant—the "my scar is longer than your scar" way of praying. You are an ambassador of the Lord, and the supplicant needs to focus on the Lord, not on your own concerns, even when they are offered with all good intentions of sharing the burden of suffering and conveying your understanding. We need to get out of God's way, and let God act as he sees fit.

Many come to healing prayer in fear; fear is the opposite of love. When the fear is a block to God's healing grace, sometimes that grace can be received by osmosis during the ministry we call "soaking prayer." Soaking in prayer is a time to allow the peace of God that passes all understanding to gently wash over us and fill us with peace. In soaking prayer people lie on the floor for some time—perhaps two hours—in a place that is filled with prayer. Some even fall asleep. Scripture is read, and the healing grace of God fills those who are in need, as if the word is permeating the skin and going right to the point of pain. The person is surrounded by love, grace, peace, and the word of God soaking through the outer layer of thick skin to the very heart of the issue, right into the wound, the scar tissue, the disease. Healing can be found in the release of fear.

When praying for inner healing, or the healing of memories, at this point the supplicant is asked to close her eyes, to place her feet firmly on the ground, and to tell the story of a memory that needs healing. What follows is prayerful conversation between the supplicant and the prayer team as the story is unpacked. At a certain point, as the Lord leads, the supplicant is asked if she can see the Lord Jesus Christ at the scene of the crime. The supplicant is encouraged to look around to see the Lord, to see his reaction, his gaze, and his presence. In some cases words are exchanged. The power of the presence of the Lord in the memory is an extraordinary thing to behold.

I encourage the prayer team to keep their eyes open during inner healing because the body language of the supplicant can speak volumes in reading what is going on. This method of prayer takes practice; it is rather like holding a soul in the palm of your hand as you pray, like an egg clasped in your palm—one flinch and the egg is broken. It is a very delicate but loving way of bringing someone out of an inner torment of past hurts. The outcome is truly amazing in the realization of the power that was holding the supplicant captive. When the memory is recalled in the future, the truth is seen in Christ Jesus and the mind and body are no longer bound to respond as before.

What more should we pray? This is it! We need to ask boldly and with faith. This is what Jesus meant when he said, "Ask and it will be given to you" (Matthew 7:7). All you have to do is believe and show up; God does the rest. It has taken me years to realize that! It is all about Jesus and his love for us. Get yourself out of the way and watch God at work. You will be awed by the mystery of the healing ministry.

Finally, in order to receive healing we have to say "Yes and amen" to God. We have to be open to God, even just a little; we have to accept the fervent prayers of others. It is an amazing thing to see the moment of acceptance, like a jigsaw puzzle piece falling right into place. It all makes sense.

To accept the healing can be a hurdle, but what do we do when we are given a gift? We say thank you. Thanking God is so important. Having an attitude of gratitude and thanksgiving is vital to the healing ministry. We do not always see instantaneous healing. We pray in confidence that the seed has been planted and is growing, and that God himself is nurturing that seed. Our gratitude is the start of receiving the gift from God.

How about standing firm in your faith that Jesus meant what he said when he told his disciples they would "place their hands on sick people, and they will get well" (Mark

16:18)? That is something to start with, is it not? Start at home. Start with a family member. Start with something simple like a headache—but pray. First, ask: May I lay my hands on you? Don't be discouraged if nothing seems to happen at first. Pray again; even Jesus prayed twice for the blind man! Take that step out of the boat, keep your eyes on the Christ, do not let your faith waver. And do not worry about the outcome: that is up to God. Do your best and God will do the rest! Do your part in believing, try less and trust more. Let God work through you. In giving we receive, and I pray that you will be encouraged to do what Jesus taught us to do. I pray that you will join me in being a witness to this resurrection of the forgotten touch. In all humility, in all faith, in all trust, in all holy boldness, in all love, in all peace, stretch forth your hand to heal in the name of Jesus. What is stopping you?

CHAPTER 10

No Hands But Our Hands
Caring for the Caregiver

*If you spend yourselves on behalf of the hungry and
satisfy the needs of the oppressed, then your light will
rise in the darkness, and your night will become like
the noonday. The LORD will guide you always; he
will satisfy your needs in a sun-scorched land and
will strengthen your frame. You will be like a well-
watered garden, like a spring whose waters never
fail. (Isaiah 58:10–11)*

The cities of Coventry, England, and Dresden,
Germany, were very badly bombed during World War
II. Youth from both cities went to help each other rebuild.
In cleaning out a church that had been bombed in

Dresden, a statue of our Lord on the cross was found in the rubble. The figure and the cross were unscathed, but both of Jesus' hands had been blown off. Both of them! The church was rebuilt and the cross was put back, but the hands were not replaced. A plaque was positioned at the foot of the cross with the words, *Ohne Deine Haende, habe ich keine Haende*—or, "I have no hands but your hands."

Take a look at your hands. What do you see? How do you use your hands in service to the Lord? What are you doing to help others? How can your hands be Christ's hands for others? Are you called to remind people of what Jesus taught in praying for this resurrection of the forgotten touch?

It is such a privilege to pray for others. It is such a joy to hear and see what God does as he heals. Sometimes it feels euphoric and exhilarating—Wow, God is really doing something here!—and it is so exciting to watch God at work. But any book on the healing ministry would not be completely honest if it did not acknowledge that there are other times when it is all just totally exhausting. Sometimes I feel like the very bone marrow of my being has been removed and I have nothing left to give. I do not like feeling like that, but over the years I have learned the very good news that when we are weak the Lord is strong.

In the gospel story about the woman who suffered a hemorrhage for twelve years, Jesus turned to the crowd and asked, "Who touched me?" when the woman was healed. The disciples thought it strange he would ask such a question, since the crowd was pressing on him, but Jesus told them that he knew a healing had taken place: "Someone touched me; I know that power has gone out from me" (Luke 8:46). When we pray for healing power leaves the person who is praying; is it any wonder that we are drained after hearing the burdens of others and praying for their healing?

Once when I was at a low ebb and feeling completely depleted, Canon Jim Glennon reminded me that a reservoir needs to be refilled. He asked me if I was drawing on the sludge at the bottom of the reservoir or drawing on the sweetness of the overflow. In other words, he was telling me I needed to refill the reservoir, and indeed to make sure I was keeping it full at all times. The preflight instructions from an airline stewardess are poignantly clear: "Place the oxygen mask on your own face first and then on the child." This is not a selfish act: it is common sense. And we in the healing ministry need to do the same.

As a prayer minister for healing one needs to be very open to the Holy Spirit. Jennifer Larcombe wrote: "As you pour out I will pour in, like a drain pipe. Open at the top so water pours in, open at the bottom so it pours out again. That's all we have to do! Our only responsibility is to keep the top open and the bottom open to avoid getting clogged up in the middle with rubbish." Sounds simple, but this ministry can be very draining (if you will pardon the pun). Prayer team members need to be aware that the needs and concerns of the individual who is struggling with illness can become all-consuming if one is not careful. After being with inspirational people we are energized, enthused, and fired up. Being with people who are suffering can be incredibly draining. As a caregiver and as a minister of healing it is vitally important to keep a balance. My mentor Francis MacNutt pointed out a long time ago that we need to "respond to the Spirit, not the need."

Even Jesus had to set a few boundaries in getting away from the crowds. He listened to the promptings of the Spirit and when he heard the word that it was time to spend time alone in rest and prayer, "he gave orders to cross to the other side of the lake" (Matthew 8:18). There are seven references in the gospels to Jesus crossing to the other side of the Sea of Galilee. Why was Jesus so often crossing the lake? It appears that even he needed to get away from the crowd, for the sick and needy were pressing in on him. Apparently Jesus too needed his space for rest and prayer time to be with his Father.

Rosalynn Carter once said, "There are only four kinds of people in the world: those who have been caregivers; those who are currently caregivers; those who will be caregivers; those who will need caregivers." Giving care is part of the fabric of human life. In my experience, those who care for others through healing prayer regularly need to "cross to the other side," to get away and have some peace and time for quiet. The new buzzword is "compassion fatigue," but everyone who is or has been a caregiver knows what burnout feels like, when all one has to offer has been spent and there is nothing else to give. Or perhaps we are suffering only a brown-out, a temporary cutting back on power because there is not enough power left to give, or there is an overusage of power, or too much power is draining out.

When thinking about why we experience compassion fatigue, it is good to examine what is driving us to care in the first place—guilt, resentment, anger, fear, materialism, need for approval, duty? Or love, obligation, being the only one in the family who is able to help, our geographical location? Perhaps it is a combination of these. In any case, sustaining oneself as a minister of healing is a question of balance. We need retreats and sabbaticals; we need a "time out" to recharge our batteries. Boundaries need to be set in all gentleness and compassion. Finding a spiritual director can be a great help, someone to come alongside us once a month to help carry our burden. Perhaps the key here is to remember that we are not the Christ: the burden is heavy, but the yoke is light with and through Christ (Matthew 11:30).

I have found that caregivers need to tell their story and find someone on the "other side" who will listen. Sometimes that is all that is needed, just someone to know what they are going through in caring for someone else. Guilt plays an enormous part in the burden of the caregiver. Some have told me that they have left their patient to go shopping, and after completing the mission have popped into a coffee shop to sit down and have a coffee—only to feel so guilty in taking ten minutes for themselves they cannot enjoy the break. In a week of continually giving to another, those ten minutes can be such a gift—a modern-day equivalent of crossing to the other side!

I remember hearing a story about British missionaries in Africa who employed the locals to carry their equipment. When they were pushed too hard and were told to press on to the next village too many times, they all sat down, as if on strike. They had had enough. They told the missionaries, "We have to stop and let our souls catch up with our bodies!" I think that just about sums up what care to the caregiver is all about.

Love is the greatest command, to love God and our neighbor as ourselves. As caregivers we need to log onto this. Should we minister when we are hungry, angry, lonely or tired (HALT)? Often we have no choice, but sometimes we are suffering from "servant's disease." The primary symptom is not being able to say "no." Are we prayerfully taking care of ourselves? If not, we won't be around to take care of others. Seek a balance and remember to keep giving it all over to God. We can get worn out weeping "with those who weep" if we don't balance it with rejoicing "with those who rejoice" (Romans 12:15). We need to use the gifts God has given us, so we can recognize both our strengths and limitations moving from servitude to servanthood. Perhaps the bottom line here is that there is only one Savior—and we are not him.

When we take time to "let our souls catch up with our bodies" we gain perspective; when we share our story with someone else we realize we do not have to carry this burden alone. Humor helps, too. One day I called Francis MacNutt about speaking to a thousand teenagers. I was not in a good place and was a little apprehensive. Truth be told, I was very uncomfortable. As I told Francis about my concerns he laughed. I have to say I was a little sur-prised—here I was pouring out my soul in fear and trembling, and my mentor was laughing? "Nigel," Francis finally responded, "I have two words for you. HAVE FUN." No one in my life had ever said that to me. What a novel thought for someone who has always tried to have a British stiff upper lip! Francis reminded me of his wife Judith, and how natural, kind, funny, and peaceful she is when talking to so many people. This was indeed a life-changing moment for me, as I had never in my life even imagined that fun could be a part of work!

Henry Morehouse, the nineteenth-century English evangelist, tells of the time when he was feeling loaded down with the burdens of his ministry and the Lord gave him a tender reminder of his care. When he came home one day, his young daughter Minnie, whose legs were paralyzed, was sitting in her wheelchair. He was going to take a package upstairs to his wife when his daughter asked if she could carry it. Morehouse said, "Minnie dear, how can you possibly carry the package? You cannot even carry yourself." With a smile on her face, Minnie said, "I know, Papa. But if you will give me the package, I will hold it while *you* carry me." Morehouse saw this as a picture of his relationship to God and the burdens of ministry he was carrying. Now he could proceed with confidence, knowing that the Lord was carrying him.

Whenever I give a talk or healing mission I like to start with the following passage from 1 Corinthians:

> When I came to you, brothers [and sisters], I did not come with eloquence or superior wisdom as I proclaimed to you the testimony about God. For I resolved to know nothing while I was with you except Jesus Christ and him crucified. I came to you in weakness and fear, and with much trem-

bling. My message and my preaching were not with wise and persuasive words, but with a demonstration of the Spirit's power, so that your faith might not rest on men's wisdom, but on God's power. (1 Corinthians 2:1–5)

Paul is clearly pointing to God as the healer and describing his weakness, fear, and even trembling in proclaiming this mystery. Look at his humility as he demonstrates and confesses his mere humanness. The fruit here is the "demonstration of the Spirit's power," the evidence of the power of answered prayer.

I believe that as a minister of healing and one seeking to really help others in this ministry we must pray to put on the mind of Christ and to become ambassadors for Christ: "We are therefore Christ's ambassadors, as though God were making his appeal through us. We implore you on Christ's behalf: Be reconciled to God" (2 Corinthians 5:20). The healing ministry is based on reconciliation and love, release and prayer. We all—those who come for prayer and those who are praying—need to seek to be reconciled to God and to one another. In other words, we have to be right with God and keep our balance in this walk in order to keep taking the next step and the next, in order to be in this for the distance. As my mentor Francis MacNutt would say, "Are you in this for the sprint or the long haul?" How do we "get right" with God? Seek first his kingdom and talk to someone. Confess our sins, come into his courts with thanksgiving, and put our hand in his. He has no other hands in this world but ours.

CHAPTER 11

The Church at Prayer
Planting a Healing Ministry in the Parish

Let us draw near to God with a sincere heart in full assurance of faith, having our hearts sprinkled to cleanse us from a guilty conscience and having our bodies washed with pure water. Let us hold unswervingly to the hope we profess, for he who promised is faithful. And let us consider how we may spur one another on toward love and good deeds. Let us not give up meeting together, as some are in the habit of doing, but let us encourage one another— and all the more as you see the Day approaching. (Hebrews 10:22–25)

It is worth reflecting the fact that churches with the greatest growth in the United Kingdom and the United States offer healing ministry. There is a huge need and this ministry offers faith in action. If a parish has compassion and hope and is obedient to the command of Jesus in preaching the kingdom and healing the sick, people will be drawn to share in its common life. Offering a compassionate ear and hand can help so many people and bring many to know the Lord. What would it take for your church to become a place of healing? How could you go about planting a ministry of healing in your parish?

The blocks to healing described earlier also apply to a church as a whole, especially unforgiveness and any acceptance of occult activity. Another block can be the rector or pastor: if the rector has a heart for the ministry of healing all well and good; if not, then what? Identifying those with obvious gifts of healing would be a good start. Then find a natural lay leader and perhaps others who have been healed in the past and create a team. A very slow and gradual introduction to the parish may be needed. The best place to introduce it is from the pulpit, very gently and very slowly. Perhaps the clergy or lay preachers could offer a series of homilies on the gospel healing narratives, to raise up for the congregation the fact that healing was an integral part of Christ's ministry. Teaching from the book of Acts is also helpful, as it shows the ways the early church embraced healing in its evangelism and care for the Christian community and beyond.

Once you have identified the members of a parish healing team and have gathered like-minded people alongside you, come together for an initial, informal meeting. Pray, fast, and discuss your hopes and dreams.

Keep a record of what is discussed and plan the work and then agree on how to work the plan. If at all possible, include the clergy in this meeting since it is important that they are "on board" and supportive, if not passionately and actively involved. In planting this healing ministry you will need to work with the leaders of the congregation, so anyone who needs to know about it should join you for this initial overview. The goal at this point is simply to spark that initial flame of a call in recognizing the quickening of the Spirit.

There are many ways to introduce a healing ministry to a congregation. Here, in outline form, is one approach or strategy you can adopt and adapt if you have a desire to see a healing ministry flourishing in your parish.

1) Prepare and educate yourself. Read books on healing and search the Bible for passages on healing. Ask yourself, What did Jesus mean about preaching the kingdom *and* healing the sick? (Luke 9:2). You may want to write down your thoughts so you are clear. Pray and fast. Prayer is essential. Ask God, "Do you want me to do this ministry?" Remember that you are not the first person to start a healing ministry at a church, so find a mentor and be creative. Reach out for help and visit other churches who have had this ministry in place for some time. You do not need to re-invent the wheel! In all that you do, be an encourager, inspire the shared vision, model the way, enable others to act, and be available. Pray, pray, and

pray some more. Be aware of your personal life and keep it in order. Be accountable to your rector or pastor, and find a supervisor or spiritual director. You must not feel alone as you step out of the boat in faith. Fear and worry about what others are thinking may discourage you; the team approach can help you know that you are not alone.

2) Have a meeting with the pastor or rector in order to understand his or her views on the healing ministry and to make sure you are on the same page.

3) Identify those in the parish with obvious gifts for healing. Reread 1 Corinthians 12 and go through a parish list, writing beside the names the gifts that you see in each parishioner who might be called to this ministry. Contact like-minded people and people who you know have been healed in the past. Those who have been healed of cancer, for example, have great compassion and understanding and sometimes even healing gifts for those who have been recently diagnosed. Confidentiality will be an essential part of this ministry and should be evaluated carefully, along with the motivation of candidates. Ask possible candidates, "Why do you want to be part of a healing prayer team?"

4) Identify a leader and core prayer team. The prayer team could be led by the clergy, but do not assume this should be the case. A spark of genuine desire and enthusiasm is essential, and not all clergy have gifts for healing. The healing team leader should be sensible, upstanding, and faithful, and like the team members, should be able to listen, love, and pray.

Prayer team members should have a teachable spirit, and the ability to learn from others and take their suggestions gracefully. Consider questions such as: How long should someone be on the team? How would we remove someone from the team, if necessary?

5) Begin gathering for prayer weekly. Fast and work out the plan. Start prayer team training by reading books and studying Christian Healing Ministry CDs, levels one, two, and three. Meet regularly, perhaps weekly or monthly. As this small community is gathering and studying, learn to be comfortable offering prayer for others by praying for each other. Invite guest speakers—doctors, nurses, clergy, lay ministers of healing, people who can share their story of being healed—to help you learn discernment, and to guide you in your studies. Make sure that at some point the prayer team is put through a program addressing sexual harassment. This is vitally important in offering a safe ministry. The church offers programs in harassment training and all the prayer team should have a certificate to show that they have taken the course. It is also important to help prayer team members understand that dying is very much a part of the healing ministry. Read books on death and dying, and bring in speakers who can educate team members about the role of healing in the midst of death and grieving. Debriefing with the prayer team after each death will be important.

6) Ask the clergy or lay preachers to lead a series of homilies or educational classes on healing, as a gentle

introduction to the healing ministry. There are so many stories of healing in the gospels, in Acts, and in the Old Testament. Have fun exploring what the Bible has to say on the subject.

7) When the team is ready, begin offering healing prayer either in the pews right after Sunday services or at the time of communion. Prayers for healing can be said right after a parishioner has received communion, or parishioners can be invited to move to a separate place for prayer during communion, or to come back at a later time during or after the service.

8) Consider helping the clergy in visits to homebound parishioners and those in nursing homes and hospitals. Your rector or pastor may be grateful for a pastoral team to lessen the load. Or perhaps one or two of the team could go with the rector on visits, expanding the gifts of the church by offering effective, prayerful, and compassionate ministry to those in need.

9) When a group of prayer team members have completed their training or reached a certain benchmark in their studies, I would suggest commissioning them in a service that includes the anointing of the hands that will be stretched forth in faith. This can be done when the bishop visits, or during any Sunday service.

10) Spread the word. Consider offering an ecumenical healing service and invite everyone in your village, town, or city to your church. Invite likeminded clergy from other denominations to join you. (See the next chapter for ideas on healing services.)

Also consider inviting a "known name" to your church to jump-start the ministry. This always creates an interest and the fruit of such a visit can really set a fire of hope and encouragement.

11) Always debrief at each meeting. What is working? What is not? Should we do it again? After each step ask God for direction, knowing that he will guide you. Keep the flame lit by offering programs, inviting speakers, providing further training. Monthly gatherings of the prayer team can be fun—try potluck dinners or afternoon teas. Prayer with community builds a church and builds up faith.

12) Keep a record of answered prayer right from the start, even the "ingrown toenail" stories. Keeping such a record can be wonderful for many reasons, especially when the honeymoon is over and discouragement has a go with you. Read the success stories and testimonies as encouragement.

As you see this healing ministry in the parish take root and grow, there are a number of prayer team pitfalls and dangers to be aware of and to watch for:

1) Prayer team accountability during prayer is vitally important. Some people can get carried away. Teach the prayer team to tap a team member three times as a signal to redirect his or her prayer. This non-public redirecting can be very positive and keep the prayer team Christ-centered.

2) Be very aware of gossip. Gossip is absolutely not permissible and will destroy a vibrant healing ministry. If a parishioner confides in the prayer team and the concern is leaked to the congregation, that person's confidence in healing prayer will be compromised and the news will spread that the prayer team is not to be trusted. Be very careful not to invite gossips to the prayer team, and to confront any violation of confidence swiftly and firmly. Gossip is just not allowed. Here is a test: If you are not part of the problem and you are not part of the solution, it is gossip!

3) Be careful of the "my scar is bigger than your scar" attitude. Train the prayer team members to be compassionate and focused on listening, loving, and praying for others, and not to offer stories of their wounds from the past except on those rare occasions when they are valuable means toward healing.

4) Similarly, watch out for the "misery loves company" attitude. A spirit of discouragement and self-pity may be lurking underneath; be prayerful about this.

5) Be attentive to those who need deliverance ministry, especially those who might "act out" at the Holy Eucharist or healing service. It is best to have a plan for how to handle disruptive people, perhaps removing them to a room away from the church in order to avoid the possibility of a crowd forming. Take charge and with authority tell the supplicant to quiet. Do not start a deliverance ministry if you have not had any training in it. I would suggest that you

"bind the issue" in Jesus' name before proceeding, and then get help. Refer the supplicant to someone with expertise in this area, if needed.

6) Be very careful not to make any of the prayer services a theatrical performance. A quiet, gentle setting is desired. No waving of the hands or loud prayers that only call attention to the one who is praying.

7) Be aware of prayer team burnout and the importance of setting boundaries. "No" is a complete sentence. Check in with the team members regularly as to how they are managing the burdens. Remind them to be careful in giving out their home phone numbers—very needy people will call at all times of the day and night. Also be aware of the "drowning man syndrome," in which one person in need begins to drag others under the water with him. Set boundaries well.

Starting a healing ministry from scratch is like the chicken and the egg quandary. Do you train the healing team in preparation for the healing services, or do you have a healing service and see what grows out of it? Would it be good to train the team, open the door, and see who comes? Or should we move very slowly, learning to crawl, walk, and run before settling into a steady jog on the road leading others to the healing love and compassion of our Lord? There is no right or wrong answer, and each parish will follow a different path depending on its circumstances and leadership. The important thing is that you get started, trusting that the Lord will indeed bring amazing fruit to your efforts if you pray with faith—even faith as small as a mustard seed.

CHAPTER 12

Ask, Seek, Knock

Introducing the Healing Service

Ask and it will be given to you; seek and you will find; knock and the door will be opened to you. (Matthew 7:7)

In the previous chapter I suggested a strategy for planting a ministry of healing in a congregation. In this chapter we will focus specifically on several ways prayer for healing can be introduced to a congregation.

After several sermons on the subject of healing have been offered, it may be time to begin offering a "pew ministry" of healing prayer. A couple of members of the newly formed healing prayer team could sit at a certain pew set aside for quiet prayer after the Sunday services. (The pew needs to be relatively private, either at the front of the church or at the back, whichever is away from the line to the exit or the route to the coffee!) If someone has had some bad news that week they could go to the team members and tell them what happened, and then they would pray. I have found this to be a gentle way of introducing the kindness of Christ in addressing a need.

The next step perhaps would be to offer the laying on of hands at the communion rail after the Holy Eucharist has been received. Those wanting this ministry can stay behind after receiving the bread and wine, so that a member of the prayer team will be alerted to go to them and offer prayer. Another method is to have a prayer station or two available, strategically located so as to allow access to healing prayer for those who have just received communion.

After these ministries are in place, your church may be ready to try a full healing service. In preparing for these services it is good to invite the local community to join you. At some point you may also decide to invite clergy from other denominations; it can be a wonderful way of knocking down the walls of denominational boundaries. Give them a part in the service; this will help to create a healing community without walls. It would be worth considering inviting a well-known speaker, either to jump-start the ministry or to give a boost after a year or so of experience in the healing ministry. Consider offering a healing mission: a Friday night presentation, Saturday with talks and small groups ending with a healing service at 3 P.M. or 4 P.M., and then offering the pulpit to the speaker on Sunday, so that those who did not come to the mission are given a taste of Jesus' healing. You might consider offering the healing ministry during that Sunday service as well.

Whenever you decide to hold the service, hymns and/or praise and worship start the service, a word of welcome is offered, and then testimony of prayers answered and healings received can be offered and drawn out of the congregation. I find quoting Acts 13:15 helpful here: "If you have a message of encouragement for the people, please speak." This form of prayerful conversation with the congregation can be extremely helpful in building one's faith. It takes a lot of courage on behalf of the clergy or leader of the service to invite these testimonies, because there is often a time of blank space during which the silence can grow uncomfortable. If you can draw them out to tell of the great things God has done, a deeper relationship within the community is built, both for those who speak and those who hear. It offers a chance for the people to proclaim and receive the living gospel for today. When asking for testimony set up clear guidelines, saying something like: "We want to hear what Jesus has been doing in your life, how he is healing today. This is not a time for a sermon or complaint—save that for the narthex! This is not a time to sell products such as some amazing diet pill that has helped you lose weight. We want to hear what Jesus is doing today in your life. What message of encouragement do you have?"

After all who wish to speak have done so, a gradual hymn is sung, Scripture is read, and a homily or teaching on the ministry is presented. Then anointing and the laying on of hands is offered. This is where the prayer team jumps in. I would suggest that you bring the prayer team forward, stand in a circle with hands joined, and lead a prayer encouraging the prayer team to "listen, love, and pray." Remind them that they will have a soul in their hand for a brief moment, ask them to pray with all their heart, mind, body, and soul. The prayer teams should consist of at least two people, with no more than four on a team. Sometimes I like to draw a particular person from the congregation, one who is very ill, perhaps. I then invite the whole congregation to lay hands on this person (very lightly) and I lead a prayer of healing for that person. This way a corporate body of Christ is created and we all get to pray. I always anoint the hands of the attending spouse or caregiver as well.

A team of a man and a woman is best for the bulk of the prayer teams; however, I do like to offer a prayer team for women only and one also for men only—two women on one team and two men on another. I like to put the prayer teams at the back or sides of the church if possible, since people who have been prayed for often cry, and they do not want to turn and face the whole congregation with "messed up mascara." Putting the prayer teams away from the front of the church offers compassion and a measure of privacy. The clergy or the preacher or the bishop (if present) could stand at the crossing or the front of the aisle and anoint those who desire prayer first and then send them to the prayer teams strategically scattered around the back and sides of the church.

Oftentimes the guest speaker is deluged by a rush of people in need, and it is important to set boundaries.

When I am the guest speaker in services where there are more that seventy-five people, I like to anoint the supplicant and say a very brief prayer as the Spirit leads. Sometimes the Lord gives me a word of knowledge for the individual. The congregation is instructed not to speak to me, but to speak only to the prayer teams. If every member of the congregation were allowed to tell their stories the service would go on for hours and hours! So I anoint, place my hand on the head, back, or shoulders of the supplicant, and pray from my heart, trusting God to give me the words.

I would suggest that the prayer team members always directly ask, "Hello, what is your name, and how may we pray for you?" Then listen with your eyes, ears, and body. You have a soul in your hand, pay attention. Do not let your eyes drift to another prayer team! That suggests rejection. Pay attention, concentrate, *really* listen. Remember to smile and look people in the eye, and to weep with those who weep if you are so moved. Clarify anything that you are not sure of and then pray the history of what you have just heard. *Never* compare your wounds with those of the supplicant!

Not all the prayer team members need to pray out loud; you can take turns if you wish. If you feel there is a need for follow-up, suggest it to the supplicant. Do not forget about salvation; remember this may be a moment to bring someone to know the risen Lord. Plant the seed of healing and let it go. Allow God to do what he does best. You do the asking, as Jesus commanded; God does the healing and all the praise goes to him. As a surgeon once said to me, "Nigel, I change the dressing, God heals the wound." If a supplicant expresses gratitude to you, remind him or her that God is the healer, not you!

The service is concluded with a hymn, a blessing, and the dismissal. It is a good practice for the prayer team members to gather and say a "cutting-free prayer" after the service so that they do not take anything home with them except the perfect love of Jesus. A period of debriefing might be in order a couple of days later—or, if an issue is pressing, right there and then. It is good to have a discussion of what worked and what did not work so that changes can be made next time. This ministry is extremely emotional and therefore extremely tiring, especially if you are an introvert. Allow time after the service to rest, since you may be exhausted. I often feel completely and utterly drained after a healing service. Go home and take care of yourself. Allow time to rest after such walking on the waters by faith.

If healing services are an entirely new experience for a congregation, it might be helpful to offer instruction about what to expect and how to prepare for the service. This can be done in a parish newsletter or perhaps in a sermon prior to the healing service. You might encourage people who are thinking about coming to the healing service in the following way.

> First, we encourage you to spend some time in prayer. Jesus said, "Ask," so what you will be doing is asking, making your request known to God. Go to the service with an intention. You are not doing

anything new—this has been done for at least two thousand years! Perhaps you feel nervous or self-centered; many people do. Just showing up is nine-tenths of the work! Give your soul a gift and take yourself to a gentle healing service. Let us give you permission to sit in the back pew; many are healed even there. In fact, you need not even speak of your concern if it is too personal. When asked, "How may I pray for you?" you can respond, "God knows my concerns"—because he does! You are going to receive the love of God and the healing grace of God, even if you do not think that you are worthy. We have some good news for you: you are worthy because of Jesus Christ. We do encourage you to go forward to receive prayer, even if you are shy and introverted. Go on, stand up and ask. Go for it. Go up and receive the love of God you deserve.

Now, here is the key. When we receive something, we have to do something, something very simple. We must say three words: "Thank you, God." You do not even have to thank the prayer team, but please be sure you thank God. Thank him for the healing that has been planted in your person through people of faith and those that truly believe, with all their heart, mind, body, and soul.

If you have never attended a healing service, we urge you to step out of your comfort zone, to step out of the boat in faith, and take your burden to the foot of the cross with compassionate people who believe for you and with you. The prayer team members have a giving heart and will "believe for you," even if your faith is as small as a mustard seed.

If the members of your congregation have not witnessed speaking in tongues or resting in the Spirit before the healing service, this might be a little disconcerting the first time they see it, if indeed it happens at that healing service. Again this is nothing new, but it may be new to them. The gift of tongues, in my opinion, is the ability to let our soul pray in groans: "We do not know what we ought to pray, but the Spirit himself intercedes for us with groans that words cannot express" (Romans 8:26). Perhaps, just perhaps, it is our soul speaking. Now that is something to ponder!

Resting in the Spirit is also a truly amazing gift from the Holy Spirit. The first time it happened when I was praying with someone it seemed a "little freaky," but now I can usually tell when it will happen. The supplicant often starts to sway in place with eyes closed, and then leans backward and falls gently to the floor. I always make sure I have a "catcher" in place behind the supplicant, though sometimes people just drop in place. I view resting in the Spirit (or "carpet time") as a heavenly anesthetic, a peace that passes all understanding. When we are in such peace, God performs the surgery!

Prior to the service, the prayer team members need to teach a couple of strong-backed people how to catch supplicants who are resting in the Spirit. Have them close their fists and carefully put their arms forward under the armpits of the supplicants. Then very gently lower them to the ground. Try not to let them bounce, and consider cradling the head so it will not hit the stone floor of the church! You might wish to have pillows and small modesty blankets available.

If someone rests, leave him or her there. Encourage people to stay on the floor and not to get up too fast. The catchers, if available, should also help people back to their feet when they are ready. Unless they are sobbing or seem in distress, it is fine to leave them on the floor having a personal moment with God. You do not need to interfere. If they are crying, then it might be good to kneel or sit beside them and offer comfort as needed. Tears will flow when wounds are healed; they are a quite normal sign of the presence of the Holy Spirit. I remind people that our tear ducts are a gift from God, so feel free to use them! It is interesting to note that tears of sadness and tears of joy have a different chemical make-up. Different toxins are released from your body when you cry, depending on the reason behind the tears. Thank you, God for the holy gift of tears. Many people have said to me, "Nigel, I am worried that if I start to cry I will never stop." Perhaps it is time to cry to continue your walk of healing.

A Checklist for a Healing Service

1) Healing service or an informal gathering with prayer?

2) Location of service: church, hospital, chapel, home?

3) Ecumenical or local congregation only?

4) Preacher: guest speaker? clergy? lay leader? doctor? nurse?

5) Publicity?

6) Elements of the service: hymns? readings? sermon/homily? testimonies? Eucharist? When to offer the laying on of hands?

7) Prayer teams: Who? Leader? Roles? Where the teams will stand? How will a need for deliverance or other possible disturbances be handled?

8) Refreshments: coffee hour? dinner?

9) Post-service meeting: discussion of what worked, what did not. How will follow-up be handled? Who will take phone calls? Plan for another service? Weekly, monthly, annually?

Epilogue

If my people, who are called by my name, will humble themselves and pray and seek my face and turn from their wicked ways, then I will hear from heaven and will forgive their sin and will heal their land. (2 Chronicles 7:14)

During a large healing service several years ago I suddenly saw a man in a purple shirt and clerical collar standing in front of me. This bishop said in a very strong Irish accent, "Good evening, Nigel. Would you pray for me and my country?" It was all I could do not to go into post-traumatic stress mode. I prayed and asked him if could I see him after the service. We had a good chat. I had not yet discovered that the companion diocese to the diocese of Albany, where our healing center is located, is County Down and Dromore, which includes the city of Belfast, Northern Ireland. In 1974 I had vowed that Belfast was one place in the world to which I would never return. I had assured myself there was no chance I would ever have to revisit that city, a place filled with horrible memories of violence and untold suffering. Obviously God had a different idea! Sometimes God's sense of humor fills me with laughter. You want me to do *what*, Lord?

After that initial meeting, Bishop Harold Miller asked me over a period of three years to come to Belfast. Each time I said I would pray about it—that seems to be the standard reply for major quandaries! It bought me time and I was able to shelve the question several times, hoping it would go away. I prayed and prayed, knowing that I should go but also knowing, quite frankly, that I did not want to go. As someone once wisely noted, a person who has been raped does not wish to go back to the scene of the crime. I felt so uncomfortable even thinking about the trip that I would break out in cold sweats at night. I was so dreadfully wounded emotionally by my experiences in 1972, 1973, and 1974; I was full of memories that needed healing.

One day I told my bishop that I simply could not go. The next day Bishop Bill said, "I am going to Ireland. Would you like to join me?" To make a long story short, a few weeks later we were on the plane. I sat next to two chaps who were obviously terrorists and seemed terribly uncomfortable. When I asked them what they did, they were very evasive, so when they asked me what I did, I simply told them I am a priest and left it at that. Halfway over the Atlantic I asked them what they *really* did. They told me that they were Royal Marines. "What?" I was so shocked—a Sergeant Major and a Color Sergeant. Good

Lord, God has his hand on this trip, I thought. We had a wonderful chat, "swinging the lamp," as we call it.

While we were in Belfast, Bishop Harold asked me to preach at the synod (diocesan convention). I was privileged to speak to the gathered clergy of County Down and Dromore. After that homily I was totally soaked, covered with sweat from head to toe. Following the service many people came up to me, including three women who were former nurses and who had been at the Royal Victoria when my friend Tim was shot in 1972. Another woman told me that her husband was murdered by the IRA in 1972. It was all very moving.

A wonderful man who has been praying for reconciliation for forty years, Brother David Jardine, took me on a trip around Belfast, visiting some of the places where I had witnessed man's inhumanity to man. The memories were so strong, I nearly lost my breakfast at one of the sites. Much had changed over time, but I was able to locate several places that had a strong hold over my memory. At one point David and I bought two coffees and sat down next to a very large plate glass window. I started to sweat and asked if we could move. A soldier knew to avoid large windows like the plague, because when a bomb went off the glass would become flying razor blades and rip people apart. I had seen that bloody mess far too often. Instead, David prayed and I was fine.

Going back to those places was so revealing, so healing. This captive was set free. Thirty-three years ago my uniform was a flack jacket and green beret or tin hat, and I carried a 7.62 rifle. Now I went to these "hot spots" in my new uniform—a clergy collar—and I carried a Bible. As I entered one particular community one of the locals tipped his hat to me, acknowledging that I was a priest. It was as if an angel was there waiting for me and welcoming me back, which brought tears to my eyes. I think it was at that moment I felt an overwhelming love for the Irish. All those years of pain that had indeed been multiplied in my mind, just went. A dark cloud went out of my body.

> "I will bring you back from captivity. I will gather you from all the nations and places where I have banished you," declares the LORD, "and will bring you back to the place from which I carried you into exile." (Jeremiah 29:14)

I even had the chance to visit the grave of St. Patrick, where I knelt and prayed for this man who had come back to the land where he had once been a slave. I felt a certain affinity to him, and finally a deep peace. Now I can even pull my curtains closed at home and not think that a sniper is waiting out there. Strange how memories need to be healed.

On the flight back to New York I sat next to a chap who had been born a block from one of the police stations at which I was based the second month that I was in Belfast. He took great pride in telling me that he had put the eye out of a policeman by throwing a stone through a very small window at the guard house. He was so proud of himself. That was then, this was now, and here we were both reminiscing and chatting like we were old friends. My heart filled again with a brotherly love that I would not have imagined possible. I glimpsed what Jesus meant when he said, "Love your enemies."

Today, I am a new man. The Lord has created in me a clean heart and set me free from the physical and emotional wounds of the early 1970s. I am a new creation. The inner vows I had made never to return have been forever broken, and by returning to "those places" where such trauma happened I have been set free. Through Christ all things are possible. I know that I will be returning to lead healing missions in Belfast.

Recently I spoke at a Fishnet Conference to about five hundred people, and at the end I asked all those who were Irish to stand up. About three-quarters of the audience stood. As a British man I asked them to forgive me for what the British did to the Irish. The outpouring of tears was amazing. Grown men were breaking down and sobbing. So many people came up to me and told me that their mum or dad had told them to hate the British. I got soaked in tears that night. The fruit of the visit to Belfast.

❖

Finally, thank you for reading this book. I do hope and pray that you found it helpful and healing, and that you could relate to some of the stories. Please do not let this book gather dust on your shelves; when you've finished reading it, lend it to someone else. We all need to remember that we are witnessing in our generation a resurrection of the forgotten touch.

God bless you. I pray that the healing love and compassion of Jesus will be with you. I pray abundant blessings upon you as you are led to explore this most remarkable ministry. Be well, do good works, and for God's sake love one another. May the healing grace and love of Jesus be with you, with power and with signs following. *Amen.*

CX06775

15.00
7.50